7 STEPS TO HEALING FROM A TOXIC RELATIONSHIP

IDENTIFY AND OVERCOME NARCISSISTIC ABUSE, LET GO OF CODEPENDENCY, DISCOVER YOUR INNER STRENGTH, AND EMPOWER RECOVERY

EMBER BENNETT

CONTENTS

INTRODUCTION

It's easy to lose ourselves when looking for love. We all want the fairy tale—the perfect love story of living happily ever after —but unfortunately, this could lead to us being caught up in a web of manipulation and lies if we become involved with the wrong person.

Did your relationship begin as a whirlwind romance, the love story you always dreamed of, but it soon became a nightmare? That's the unfortunate reality for people who have become entangled with narcissists.

The narcissist's true colors usually emerge after the fantasy of the first phase of the relationship starts to subside. Whereas before, you were the center of their universe, they'll now begin to devalue you through manipulation and emotional abuse. They chip away at your self-esteem, confusing you and questioning your sanity.

The narcissist will take you on a nerve-wracking and bewildering journey that will reduce you to a shadow of your former self. Where they cherished you before, they will now devalue and blame you for everything that goes wrong in their lives.

Why and how do so many of us become trapped in these emotionally tumultuous relationships? The narcissist is a master of illusion who mercilessly preys on empathetic and nurturing people. Those of us who are compassionate and enjoy caring for others usually believe that love can conquer all. We believe that we can fix these broken people. However, it's these qualities that the narcissist will exploit mercilessly.

In your journey to healing and finding yourself again, you must acknowledge this painful truth: Your partner is an abusive narcissist. They have always been one and will never change, as they have no self-awareness and are incapable of change. There were signs, but they were concealed beneath the initial charm and adoration. As Adria Hagg, a therapist specializing in narcissism, aptly observes, "In relationships, narcissists often begin by idealizing their partner" (Boudin, 2021). You feel like the star of their world, showered with affection and admiration. You find out too late that it's not the start of a magical, lifelong love story but only the beginning of a tragedy.

You might be overwhelmed and sad and not see a way out of your emotional prison. But there is hope. This book aims to guide you through the maze and to be your beacon in the darkness of selfish chaos.

You'll embark on a journey of self-discovery and, ultimately, freedom. As you work through the eight steps in the book, each step will take you closer to breaking free from narcissistic abuse and rediscovering your authentic self. The tools that you gain will help you forge a path toward healthier, more fulfilling relationships.

The eight steps are as follows:

- Step 1 is about confronting the reality that your partner is an abusive narcissist. You will learn how to recognize a narcissist.
- In Step 2, you'll learn more about conquering codependency. What are the symptoms, and how can you be less codependent?
- Step 3 is about breaking free and embracing freedom and healing. Please write a letter to your narcissistic partner and end their relationship. Please do your best to put them out of your mind. You might still feel attached to them, but realizing they'll never change is essential, and you're ultimately not responsible for them.
- In Step 4, you'll reclaim your lost identity, strength, and self-worth. You'll rebuild your self-esteem and confidence after leaving the narcissist.
- In Step 5, you'll learn more about setting boundaries and why they are essential.
- Step 6 is about overcoming the challenges of recovery and how to deal with CPTSD.
- In Step 7, you'll learn how to thrive and prosper in new relationships. What does a healthy relationship look like?

- Bonus Step 8 shows you how to protect yourself from your ex.

So, are you ready to confront your reality and embrace your healing journey? It's time to begin your transformation from victim to survivor.

STEP 1: CONFRONTING REALITY – YOUR PARTNER IS AN ABUSIVE NARCISSIST

Relationships with narcissists are held in place by the hope of a "someday better," with little evidence to support it will ever arrive.

— RAMANI DURVASULA

This is Naomi's story. She was ensnared by a manipulative narcissist who kept promising her that things would change and that they would have a better life together.

I met an exciting and charismatic man two years ago who greatly impressed me. He cast a spell over me by showering me with affection and admiration. I thought we would be together for the foreseeable future and secretly hoped we would never be separated.

After being alone for so long, it felt like all my dreams were coming true, and my perfect love story had been written in the stars.

After the first two months or so, things started to change. We started disagreeing on things, which is typical for any relationship, but then, one night, while we were arguing about something trivial, he exploded. His words were literally like daggers as he cut me apart with them.

I couldn't believe that he could change so suddenly. I didn't recognize him any longer. He was very different from the person who I fell in love with.

He made me feel cherished at the beginning of the relationship, but as time passed, he became increasingly critical of my behavior and everything about me. Everything from how I dressed to the food I enjoyed and my family and friends became unacceptable to him. I slowly started to believe everything he said, and my self-esteem disappeared.

He finally managed to isolate me from most of my friends and some of my family members. He led me to believe he was the only one who cared about me.

He kept me emotionally unbalanced by showering me with love and then having an anger tantrum about something insignificant I supposedly did wrong. Shortly afterward, he would beg for my forgiveness and promise me that he would change. I would forgive him, time after time, believing things would improve.

Things worsened, as he threatened to hurt himself or ruin my life if I ever left him. I felt trapped and finally started losing my sense of self. I had to always walk on eggshells around him, trying to avoid triggering another rage episode.

One day, I looked at my tired face in the mirror, and I had to admit I wanted my life back. I wanted a life free from constant fear and my self-respect back.

Looking back, I can see how he has trapped me with his manipulation and emotional abuse. I started to rebuild my life, and going to therapy made me realize his behavior didn't reflect my worth but reflected his issues. I'm grateful that I managed to get the strength to do so.

Ultimately, my resilience got me through, and the support of family, friends, and a professional therapist helped me see the light and regain my worth. It was a grueling experience, but I learned much from it and won't make the same mistake again.

WHAT IS NARCISSISTIC ABUSE?

Have you been in a relationship like this? Maybe it started as your most affectionate relationship, and you thought you finally met the perfect partner, who could potentially be your "one."

However, after this initial love bombing stage, your relationship changed, and you soon found yourself in a special kind of emotional hell of anger outbursts, lies, manipulation, humiliation, and control. It would be best if you walked on eggshells around your former perfect partner, never quite sure what will happen.

It could feel like you're trapped in a dark room with some lurking creature that could pounce on you at any moment.

You start to realize that this person, whom you thought was so wonderful at first, is, in fact, incredibly selfish. It's almost as if they're entirely blind to your emotions and only wrapped up in their needs and desires. They have no empathy for the pain of others, and this soon becomes clear in the unfeeling comments they make when they're around you. Others who don't know them as well as you think they're simply hard on others, but you see the unpleasant truth the more time you spend with them. You're the only one there when the beast emerges behind closed doors.

Yet, even though they come across as dominant and aggressive, you know that a broken person inside them craves constant validation. However, this doesn't excuse what they're doing to you. They project their profound insecurity onto you, and you find yourself trapped in a twisted cycle of power and vulnerability.

You're a victim of a never-ending loop of abuse, a constant rotation between heavenly and hellish moments. At the beginning of the relationship, they will idealize you and make you feel like you're the center of their universe. However, then the abuse starts, and so do the reconciliation cycles. These cycles create a trauma bond that feels almost impossible to break, even when the experience becomes excruciatingly painful.

Recognizing the Narcissist

Identifying a narcissist may sound like a challenging puzzle, but the pieces will fall into place once you know what to look out for. While we all have our imperfections, understanding narcissists and being able to identify them can protect your well-being and mental health.

Controlling behavior is a red flag. If they constantly need things to go their way and your opinions don't matter to them, the person you're dealing with is likely a narcissist. If this happens in a family, the ideas and feelings usually take a backseat, and everything usually revolves around what one of the parents wants. People's voices are silenced, and their preferences don't count. In healthy relationships, everyone's opinions will matter. You must know that your feelings deserve as much respect and consideration as anyone else's.

If you're talking to someone who keeps directing the focus of the conversation back to themselves, they could be a narcissist.

They usually like the spotlight to be on them during a conversation and tend to leave other conversation partners in the shadows. Your presence is almost like a backdrop for their constant monologue. You could try sharing your thoughts and stories, but you may find them brushed aside or ignored. It's usually a case of give and take in healthy relationships, while a narcissist will hardly ask you about your day or feelings. Remember that your voice also deserves to be heard and your presence acknowledged.

Narcissists enjoy playing with your mind. They're like magicians who can leave you questioning what's real and what actually happened. While you may have a clear memory of an event, a narcissist will tell you that something didn't happen or that you are simply overreacting to something. Your view of reality is distorted, which can leave you confused and disoriented. Always trust your instincts in a relationship, and maintain your sense of self.

A narcissistic partner could try to keep you away from family and friends. You may feel like you're a prisoner behind a high wall. They'll cut you off from your support system, making you even more vulnerable to their manipulation. Remember that no one who loves you will try to isolate you from others who bring positivity and love into your life.

Narcissists love sowing seeds of doubt and making you question the intentions of others. They'll tell you that you can't trust anyone but them. They aim to plant suspicion in your mind that makes you question every interaction's authenticity. Trust is the foundation of healthy relationships. Using intuition and judgment to determine who to trust would be best.

Narcissists like to invade your privacy online. It could be likened to entering your room and looking through your belongings. They invade your digital sanctuary and peer into your thoughts without your permission. You should see your online presence as an extension of yourself and decide who you want to look into that world. You want others to respect your digital space like other parts of your life.

It's always a warning sign when they shower you with hurtful words. Communication is a bridge that connects people in a healthy relationship, touching their hearts and minds and allowing empathy and understanding to flow. However, in a relationship with narcissists, they use their words to cut you off, leaving you feeling wounded and isolated. In such a case, you must remember that you deserve to be treated with kindness and respect. Ultimately, getting out of the relationship will best protect your well-being.

If your partner threatens and intimidates you, you're going down a dangerous path.

They might use threats to control and intimidate you and try to keep you in the relationship. Trust and safety are the foundations of a healthy relationship, but threats of violence will damage your relationship and cause you to feel trapped and afraid. Safety and peace of mind are non-negotiable when it comes to a relationship. You should always put your well-being first and get away from your partner if you feel it will be better for your safety.

Narcissists wear a carefully crafted, people-pleasing mask. This is to hide their true intentions. This is the type of person you meet who's always saying and doing things that make people like them. It's a performance, and they say and do whatever they think will win people over, but there's usually a hidden agenda under their charm. You will realize that interacting with them feels very superficial, almost as if you're dealing with a character and not a genuine person.

Hoovering is a typical technique a narcissist will use to try to reel you back in if they suspect you're losing interest in them or if the relationship has ended. This involves showing them kindness and affection after they've hurt you. It's called hoovering because it's almost like they're using a vacuum to suck you back into being under their influence after they've pushed you away. You could feel caught up in a whirlwind of emotions and don't know what to expect next.

A narcissist won't respect your boundaries. Imagine you've created a safe space around yourself that you want to be respected. The narcissist will trample your boundaries, leaving them crushed and broken. It will become clear that your feelings and limits don't matter to them. Boundaries protect your emotional well-being in a healthy relationship, but you'll feel vulnerable and exposed when someone ignores them. You deserve a relationship where your boundaries and values are respected.

They also tend to control what you say and do and only allow you to say or do what aligns with their desires. This could cause you to feel suffocated as if your thoughts are trapped behind some barrier.

They will always have excuses for their bad behavior and downplay their actions. They don't take any responsibility for their behavior, and you'll be left feeling like they don't take your feelings seriously. Remember that holding someone accountable for their actions shows respect for yourself.

HOW IS A NARCISSIST CREATED?

There isn't one specific thing that leads to someone developing a narcissistic personality during childhood.

Some parents tell their children they're unique and special no matter what they do. All the child's needs are catered to immediately, making them think they're the center of the universe and deserve special treatment. They continue to believe everything must revolve around them into adulthood.

Children who are never told "no" or never face the consequences for their actions grow up thinking that rules don't apply to them and that they can do what they want.

Social media and celebrity culture have also boosted the growth of narcissism in the modern world. Some people get addicted to likes, shares, and follows. Some people copy the behavior and attitude of celebrities and then expect that they will be adored in the same way.

Some children are also never taught empathy, so they grow up not caring about what others think or feel.

On the flip side of the spoiled child, people develop narcissistic traits because they were neglected or mistreated as children. This type of personality protects them from feeling vulnerable, and they use it to shield themselves from past trauma and hide their true feelings.

So, it's not one thing that creates a narcissist, but different ingredients that make this toxic personality.

TYPES OF NARCISSISTS

Many people have ideas of what the stereotypical narcissist behaves like, but the truth is, there isn't just one type of narcissist. It can be difficult to identify them, as they appear to be so much like anyone else. Some of them, especially the covert narcissists, seem like harmless people who had complicated lives, and it may take you years to see through their victim mentality and that they don't want help but use their drama to be the center of attention. They have a reputation for being selfish, but you get narcissists who do charity work and help people or animals. They often post photos of themselves on social media where they are doing good.

Narcissism can come in different shapes and shades, and narcissists can be captivating. There is a spectrum of personalities with unique quirks and often strange behaviors. While they can initially be charming and entertaining, interacting with them becomes emotionally draining.

The Classic Narcissist

The classic, well-known narcissist is known as a "mirror gazer." They're often impeccable dressers with a penchant for admiring themselves.

They want to appear perfect to others, and their conversations often revolve around themselves and their accomplishments. They tend to bring the focus of a discussion back to themselves.

The classic narcissist will also curate every aspect of their life, from their social media profiles to their meticulously organized homes, to create an illusion of faultlessness. They want the world to see them as successful.

They have a magnetic charisma, and they draw people into their world of self-adoration. They are alluring to many people when they meet them for the first time.

The Covert Narcissist

The covert narcissist hides their self-importance behind a mask of modesty and blends in with their surroundings. They may appear introverted and harmless, but beneath their façade lies a complex and often bewildering world of manipulation.

Covert narcissists are good actors, capable of portraying themselves as unremarkable and humble individuals. They can blend into social situations, allowing them to observe and manipulate from the shadows.

They tend to use indirect tactics in their manipulation, such as passive-aggressive behavior, guilt-tripping, and even underhand compliments. They can be so discreet that you often won't be sure if you're overly sensitive or if something is wrong.

They are particularly good at gaslighting, a psychological manipulation technique that could even make you doubt your sanity. They subtly undermine your confidence and suggest that your concerns about something are exaggerated or irrational. You're left wondering if you're overreacting to something or if you should trust your instincts that something is indeed wrong.

Behind the covert narcissist's façade lies their real agenda. They want validation and admiration like their covert counterparts but pursue it more subtly. They often prefer a victim role that elicits sympathy and support from those around them.

A relationship with them is challenging because you'll be plagued by ongoing doubt. You'll often second-guess yourself and wonder if you're reading too much into a situation. This will keep you confused and may damage your confidence.

It's tough to understand them, and you need to be good at detecting subtle manipulation. You need to be able to realize that while they seemingly have a friendly personality, a more toxic reality could be hiding beneath the surface.

The Malignant Narcissist

This type of narcissist is a chilling and masterful manipulator who loves to dominate and control others. They have a dark, terrifying kind of charisma.

The malignant narcissist can exude confidence and allure, drawing people toward them like moths to a flame. This initial charm allows them to gain the trust and loyalty of those they seek to control.

Malignant narcissists enjoy chaos and turmoil. They are experts at creating and encouraging conflict, and it's within this chaos that they find their source of power, relishing the emotional turmoil they cause others, as this provides them with the validation and control they crave.

Victims of a malignant narcissist are caught in a never-ending cycle of manipulation, and they never know when the next twist in the narcissist's scheme will occur. People with malignant narcissists can experience anxiety, depression, and a pervasive dread.

Malignant narcissists can be pillars of the community, beloved by friends and colleagues, while secretly torturing their victims behind closed doors.

The Victim Narcissist

This type of narcissist is the eternal martyr of their own dramatic lives. They're excellent at playing the victim and can skillfully employ guilt, self-pity, and manipulation to control those around them.

The victim narcissist usually has an inexhaustible supply of tales that paint them as the perpetual underdog who struggles against a cruel world. They use guilt and pity as weapons and deploy these emotions strategically to manipulate the compassion of others.

For the victim narcissist, martyrdom is a way of life. The world is unfair, and they bear the brunt of its cruelty. They manipulate others through feigned helplessness. They force others to shoulder their burdens and rescue them. Learned helplessness keeps them dependent on others, and they expect constant support. They also thrive on emotional turmoil, where they can enjoy the attention of their concerned audience.

It can be challenging to escape the clutches of this type of narcissist. You have to be able to recognize their manipulative tactics, set boundaries, and refuse to play the role they want you to take in their ongoing life drama. Seek support from people who can offer you a healthier perspective.

The Social Media Narcissist

We live in the age of the social media narcissist, where selfie queens or sultans rule the web. In this digital age, a new breed of narcissism has emerged—one that thrives on the constant validation and adoration of an online audience.

These types of narcissists are masters at creating online personas. They choose the areas of their lives that they want to showcase and create their own carefully edited versions of reality. Every post they make is carefully considered.

Social media narcissists measure their self-worth by the number of followers, likes, comments, and shares they get on social media. The more likes they get, the better they feel about themselves.

They are also masters at maintaining the illusion of perfection. They use only idealized photos of themselves that have been meticulously edited and filtered. They use this to judge their worth and will also judge others by using this standard.

However, it can be exhausting to maintain this persona, and the constant need for validation can lead to depression and anxiety.

The Empathetic Narcissist

The empathic narcissist is charming and can leave their victims captivated and emotionally wounded. They can tap into the most profound emotions of others, but their intentions are usually not good.

Others are drawn to them because they are so magnetic and charismatic. What sets the empathic narcissist apart is that they understand the emotions of others. They can listen with genuine empathy and offer a shoulder to cry on. Their ability to empathize is so convincing that it can be challenging to discover their true motives.

An empathetic narcissist will exploit the vulnerabilities they uncover during their empathic interactions with you. They gather intimate knowledge about your fears, insecurities, and desires and will use this information to control you.

What makes the empathetic narcissists so formidable is that they're patient strategists. They are willing to invest time and energy in building trust and emotional intimacy with their targets. This patience allows them to cultivate deep emotional connections, which devastates their victims even more when their true intentions are finally revealed.

Life with an empathic narcissist can be confusing and emotionally unsettling. The genuine moments of connection are interspersed with confusion and doubt. Their unpredictable behavior and mixed signals can leave you questioning your reality.

It can be tricky to break free from the grip of an empathic narcissist. You must recognize the manipulation tactics hidden beneath their empathic façade and set firm boundaries.

The Somatic Narcissist

These glamor queens or kings are obsessed with their physical appearance. They believe their external attractiveness is the main reason why others admire them. However, this obsession with their own perceived beauty conceals an inner emptiness.

Somatic narcissists invest a lot of time and resources in what they perceive as maintaining peak physical perfection. They usually have a rigorous workout routine and often even undergo cosmetic procedures to become perfect.

They can also spend hours on a grooming routine, which involves anything from styling their hair to applying makeup. They always wear the latest fashions, and their clothes are perfect.

Somatic narcissists use their external beauty to protect themselves from confronting their insecurities and vulnerabilities. They are terrified of being inadequate. They're plunged into anxiety and self-doubt when they no longer receive the validation they crave.

Their relationships are often very superficial. They are more interested in how others perceive them than in deep emotional connections, and they struggle to form genuine bonds with others.

To break free from the allure of a somatic narcissist, you need to recognize that external beauty masks an inner emptiness.

The Spiritual Narcissist

This type of narcissist is a complex blend of spiritual enlightenment and egotism and conceals the true intentions behind their spirituality.

Spiritual narcissists exude an air of enlightenment and inner peace. They often engage in practices like meditation, yoga, and mindfulness, which they use as tools to project an image of spiritual depth. They use spiritual jargon and wisdom, creating an aura of transcendence.

They want followers who will worship them for their supposed spiritual powers and look up to them as spiritual guides. They often use guilt, shame, or fear to manipulate their followers into compliance, all under the guise of self-improvement and spiritual enlightenment. Their control usually seeps into various parts of their followers' lives.

These narcissists are usually driven by a powerful ego, which is at odds with the principles of humility that they preach to their followers.

Ironically, their quest for spiritual enlightenment never goes anywhere. Their focus on external validation and control prevents them from experiencing genuine inner growth and self-awareness. Their spiritual journey is just an inauthentic performance.

To break free from this type of manipulator, you must realize spiritual growth is a personal journey that someone else can't control. You must look for authentic sources of spiritual guidance.

The Intellectual Narcissist

Intellectual narcissists are self-proclaimed masters of knowledge and intellect. They often have vast knowledge but can be extremely arrogant. Engaging with them on an intellectual level can feel like stepping onto a battlefield, where victory usually means that you have to concede to their perceived superior intellect.

They believe they are more intelligent than everyone around them. They see themselves as the authority on various subjects, and they dismiss different viewpoints with a condescending air. Their arrogance is a defining feature of their personality.

Beneath their intellectual façade is a need for admiration and validation. They want recognition for their supposed wisdom and are quick to assert their knowledge in social and academic settings. Their goal is to impress others with their supposedly superior knowledge and get their admiration.

Intellectual narcissists are great at debates and philosophical discussions. They enjoy the opportunity to show off their knowledge and debating skills. Engaging with them can feel like a one-sided contest where they are determined to emerge as the undisputed victor.

Intellectual narcissists are usually also quick to dismiss alternate viewpoints. They use belittling, ridicule, or intellectual bullying to silence those who challenge their ideas. This behavior shows that they are unable to deal with dissent.

Ironically, intellectual narcissists can be so obsessed with being the most intelligent person in the room that they fail to grow intellectually in any meaningful way. They may focus on collecting facts and arguments rather than participating in meaningful intellectual exploration.

NARCISSISTIC ABUSE SYNDROME

You can develop narcissistic abuse syndrome after being mistreated by a narcissist for an extended period. It's distressing, and you can experience symptoms like dissociation, anxiety, self-doubt, and isolation.

It can be incredibly tough to deal with this type of abuse, and you could feel overwhelmed by all the challenges you have to face. You could feel like you're not there and become detached from your feelings. It seems you're experiencing events from a distance or outside your body. You could even feel as if you're dreaming.

Dissociation is a survival mechanism to deal with pain and can be a response to overwhelming stress or trauma. This is a way for your mind to cope with distress by creating a mental barrier between you and your emotions or experiences.

Another side effect of this syndrome is that you'll always feel like you're walking on eggshells. You're scared to talk freely and always think of ways to keep the person who wants to hurt you happy.

You may start to doubt yourself and wonder if you're to blame for what's happening. If you're hurt by someone supposed to care for you, it can also become difficult for you to trust others.

Some people also experience suicidal thoughts and harm them-selves to deal with the pain. You may feel ashamed and pull away from others, as you may think people could judge you if they knew what was happening. The abuse may also make you feel as if you're not good enough and give your self-confidence a knock. This could cause you to become isolated and lonely.

Narcissistic abuse syndrome will affect all levels of your health. While the abuse can leave you emotionally battered, your entire body can feel exhausted. It may feel as if the stress and pain are seeping into every corner of your body, and you could experi-ence some inexplicable aches and pains. Your immune system will weaken, and you will get sick often. Frequent headaches and digestive issues are just some health troubles you could experience.

Sometimes, when a narcissist abuses us, even the thought of becoming happy and prosperous may scare us. Narcissists are known for jealousy and quickly bring you down if they know you're happy about something. This comes from their own deep-seated need for admiration and validation from others. They can feel inadequate and insecure when someone else's positive qualities or accomplishments are highlighted.

It's possible to start believing your narcissistic abuser's lies to make sense of what's happening, even though they mostly live in their own, often strange versions of reality.

Narcissistic abuse is not only about someone being self-centered; it's also a dysfunctional behavior pattern that can leave you feeling drained and confused. Sadly, it's often a person who is supposed to care for you who destroys your confidence and makes you question your reality.

It's often difficult to recognize that you're in this type of abusive situation, and it will take time to rebuild your sense of self and create a healthier life for yourself. However, if you have the proper support, it can be done.

The Long-Term Psychological Effects of Narcissistic Abuse – Ann's Story

Ann was a talented and optimistic young woman with big dreams and hopes for the future.

When she started college, she met a charismatic man named Alex. He was charming and soon became the center of her universe. Their relationship seemed like a fairytale; he always lavished her with attention and told her how important she was to him.

However, as time passed, cracks started to appear in their relationship. Alex began criticizing her, and his comments got increasingly nasty as time passed. He mocked her appearance and made her lose confidence in her aspirations. Eventually, she didn't believe she could complete her college degree and dropped out to find a job.

Alex and Ann's relationship had become a web of control and manipulation. As the years passed, Ann became increasingly anxious. She felt nervous whenever she dared speak her mind to Alex, as she never knew what his mood would be like or what nasty words he would have to say to her. Trust, which had once been the foundation of their relationship, had long been a distant memory.

Ann had also lost most of her support network, as Alex convinced her that her friends and family were toxic. She became depressed and felt worthless. She started seeing herself as a useless disappointment.

Ann eventually got the courage to leave Alex, with the support of the friends she still had left. However, the abuse had left scars on her soul. She had nightmares about her former partner and a constant fear of running into him. Her heart even started racing when she heard his name.

Ann had to deal with post-traumatic stress and anxiety that influenced her new relationships. She questioned if anyone could be trusted. Although she was free from Alex and the abuse he inflicted on her, she found it difficult to break the cycle of self-blame and self-doubt.

Ann finally discovered her strength despite the pain she was going through. She went to see a therapist and learned to treat herself more kindly. She began to rebuild the shattered pieces of her identity, embracing her rollercoaster of emotions and letting herself feel without shame or guilt.

The effects of the abuse lingered, but Ann eventually managed to work through them and move on with her life.

NARCISSISTIC PARTNER CHECKLIST

The checklist can help you determine if you're in a relationship with a narcissistic partner. Remember that you should consider these signs in combination and not isolation, as some of these behaviors can also be present in healthy relationships. If any of these traits consistently describe your partner's behavior, finding professional support is a good idea.

Check the following characteristics to see if your partner meets any of them:

- Your partner has a great need for constant attention. They constantly seek attention, admiration, and validation from others.
- They struggle to understand or show empathy for your feelings, needs, or concerns.
- They have an exaggerated self-image. Your partner boasts about their achievements, talents, or qualities and exaggerates their importance.
- They use manipulation tactics to control and influence you or others to get what they want.
- They blame others for their mistakes. Your partner doesn't take responsibility for their actions.
- They constantly need to be validated and may get upset if criticized or unappreciated.
- They belittle or criticize you, your opinions, or your choices and undermine your self-esteem.

- Your partner acts entitled and believes they deserve special treatment without necessarily doing or giving much in return.
- They use your kindness, resources, or emotions for their gain.
- They try to isolate you from friends, family, or activities that bring you happiness and support.
- They might exhibit jealousy even in harmless situations and try to control how you interact with others. They are also jealous if you're more successful in your career than they are in theirs.
- Your partner is defensive and angry when they're criticized.
- Your partner may distort facts or change the narrative to portray themselves positively, even if it involves exaggeration or fabrication.
- The relationship feels like a constant emotional rollercoaster, with unpredictable mood swings and reactions.
- They will gaslight you, and you may start to doubt what is real. For example, did something happen, or is your memory playing tricks on you?
- Your partner places a high value on appearances and may be obsessed with their looks or social image. They're also critical of your appearance and could criticize you, for example, if you gain weight.
- They involve a third person to create jealousy, competition, or insecurity in the relationship.

Remember that this checklist is only a guide and that a professional should diagnose narcissism.

KEY TAKEAWAYS

- Relationships with a narcissist usually involve an initial love bombing or affectionate stage before the abuse starts.
- A relationship with a narcissist involves anger outbursts, manipulation, lies, control, and humiliation.
- You usually have to walk on eggshells around a narcissistic partner not to set off their rage.
- Their lies might make you feel like you're losing touch with reality.
- You will soon realize the narcissist is selfish and only wrapped in their needs and desires.
- Narcissists usually project their insecurities onto others.
- A relationship with a narcissist can involve a never-ending loop of abuse or a constant rotation between happy and unhappy moments.
- If you're unsure if someone is a narcissist, controlling behavior is usually a red flag. They always need things to be done their way.
- Many narcissists enjoy being in the spotlight and will always turn a conversation back to themselves.
- Narcissists can try to distort your view of reality, but you should trust your instincts.

- Narcissists can isolate you from your entire support network.
- They can use threats to control and intimidate their partners.
- If you fear for your well-being and safety, you must leave your partner.
- You can develop narcissistic abuse syndrome after being mistreated by a narcissist for a long time.
- This syndrome can include both mental and physical symptoms. You might blame yourself for what has happened to you and struggle to trust others.
- The abuse may have knocked your confidence and caused you to become isolated and lonely.

In the next step, we will examine codependency and how you can overcome it.

STEP 2: FACING THE MIRROR: CONQUERING CODEPENDENCY

Since narcissists deep down feel faultless, it is inevitable that when they conflict with the world, they will invariably perceive the conflict as the world's fault.

— M. SCOTT PECK

What is it like to live with a narcissist? While there can be good times, especially at the beginning of the relationship, it's primarily painful, even in life-changing ways.

Let's consider Emily's story. She spent most of her younger years living with a narcissistic partner. In the '70s, little about narcissism was known, and the charismatic man swept Emily off her feet. He showered Emily with attention and passion during the whirlwind romance.

Her parents had expressed their reservations, but Emily cut ties with her family and friends, and her life centered around her new relationship. However, her enchanting life story started to take a darker turn.

Her partner's charming exterior started unraveling, and his excessive drinking and abusive behavior shattered her ideas of their perfect love. He finally isolated her completely, manipulated her financially by living on her inheritance, and destroyed her self-esteem. Yet, she clung to the hope that things would change and that the love they once had could be revived.

However, Emily became isolated and depressed and had to start taking medication to deal with life. Her partner became increasingly verbally abusive, and she felt she couldn't escape his power.

They separated for a time, but he lured her back by promising to change, again ensnaring her with manipulation and abuse.

Emily's partner became physically violent, pushing her to the ground and breaking her ribs and nose.

She only found the strength to escape the man who had controlled and tormented her when the law intervened. She finally decided to seek help from a psychologist, realizing she needed it to save her own life.

While she worked to reclaim her life, she had to struggle to overcome the feelings of guilt and shame that were instilled in her. She still believes that not all men are like her narcissistic ex, and she wants a future where she can find healthy love.

CODEPENDENCY AND NARCISSISTIC ABUSE

Codependency can be a misunderstood and complex part of relationships.

In the early stages of codependency, you may be absorbed in your relationship with someone with narcissistic tendencies. It becomes essential, and you may deny your partner's problematic behavior. You need to please the other person and make sacrifices for them. You often give up things for them to the detriment of your well-being.

During the middle stages of codependency, you may feel a growing sense of guilt and anxiety. You question yourself and blame yourself for issues that arise. You also feel responsible for your partner's actions. There are also feelings of resentment and frustration as you realize the relationship isn't working, no matter what you do. It's overwhelming to be trapped in a never-ending cycle of trying to please someone and failing to meet their expectations.

When you're in the late stages of codependency, the rollercoaster of emotional manipulation will affect your mental and physical health. You could feel hopeless; some people turn to substances and other addictions to help them deal with their feelings.

Symptoms of Codependency

Codependency usually has the following symptoms:

- You have low self-esteem, and it's crucial that others always be satisfied with you. Your self-esteem and self-worth are fragile, and you depend on other people's opinions and validation. People-pleasing is your daily mode of living, as you live for the acceptance and approval from those around you. This can overshadow your needs and desires, which could cause you to feel a sense of emptiness you can't fill.
- Codependents usually don't have firm boundaries in their relationships. Finding a balance between giving to others and caring for your needs is difficult. It may feel more natural to react to others' feelings and thoughts. You could feel overwhelmed, and putting others first may seem the easiest option.
- It's noble to want to take care of others, but if you're codependent, this urge can go into overdrive. You could end up enabling bad behavior and taking on responsibilities that aren't yours. You could be controlling because you want to maintain stability. However, it can mask a fear of losing control.
- You likely fear rejection and always want others to approve of you. Validation can provide a temporary sense of approval and worthiness. Dependency on the support of others can create a never-ending cycle of looking for reassurance.

- You deny your personal feelings and needs and bury your painful emotions. This also becomes a way to avoid conflict and disappointment. You struggle with intimacy and dealing with relationships.

Five Steps to Stop Being Codependent

Breaking free from codependency is an act of self-love and empowerment. It would be best to start taking better care of yourself and spending less time on others.

1. First of all, stop trying to help the narcissist with everything. It's natural to want to help others, but if you're in a relationship with a narcissist who chooses to act in childlike ways, it will be used against you. Do you want to be at the beck and call of an adult who wants you to do everything for them as if they're toddlers? Like children demanding attention, a narcissist can use tantrums and drama to ensure they get their desired attention. They believe they're entitled to your attention and time.

2. Accepting that you can't change someone unwilling to change themselves is vital. So, recognize your limitations and let go. Accept that there's only so much you can do and care for yourself. Focusing on yourself and your needs at first can feel strange, but it's essential to reclaiming your sense of self. Focus on your interests, passions, and dreams. Your happiness matters, and you deserve to experience joy and fulfillment.

3. Practice being assertive and communicating your needs. It may feel strange to express your needs if you've been used to prioritizing others. Remember that assertiveness isn't about confrontation but about advocating for yourself in a way that respects your needs and the needs of others. It can help you with future, healthy interactions.

4. Say "no" to others if you don't want to or cannot do something for them. Setting boundaries is an act of self-preservation, as they are the foundation of healthy relationships. It doesn't make you selfish, but it's a way of protecting your mental well-being. Boundaries are there for you to engage with others in a way that aligns with your values.

5. Embrace self-care and self-love on your journey to healing. You should do things you enjoy and care for your mind and body. These are also essential components of your personal growth.

How Emily Overcome Codependency

Emily was a kind-hearted person who was always ready to help others. Most people in her life loved her, but there was a severe downside to her kindhearted nature. She was involved in a relationship with a narcissist, David, who didn't appreciate her and abused her in all ways possible to satisfy his needs.

She had been in a relationship with David for a few years, and everything initially seemed perfect. He was charming and charismatic, and Emily thought she had finally found the ideal man she had always sought. However, as time passed and David started revealing more of his true personality to her, she realized he wasn't a very nice person.

He had a way of making everything about himself. Even when Emily fell ill, he somehow found opportunities to be the victim when she couldn't look after him as he was used to her doing. He demanded all her attention and threw tantrums like a child to get what he wanted.

Emily always felt like she had to act very carefully around him, as she didn't want to set off his tantrums. Ultimately, her days were filled with meeting his never-ending needs and soothing his fragile ego.

She started to look for answers online. Then, one day, she found information about codependency, a subject she knew very little about. She was horrified to discover that she could see herself in the words. The article helped Emily realize that she was stuck in a cycle of trying to please David at the cost of her well-being and happiness.

Emily knew she had to break free from codependency if she wanted to change her life. She decided to break her journey away from codependency into simple steps.

Her first step was to stop doing everything for the narcissist. Emily understood that she couldn't change David, no matter how hard she tried. She decided to stop being at his beck and call, like a servant to a child. She began to set boundaries and refused to deal with his tantrums and drama.

Emily's second step was to recognize her limitations and let go. Emily accepted that there was only so much she could do to change David. She shifted her focus to self-care, nurturing her interests and passions. She realized that her happiness mattered, too.

Her third step was to practice assertiveness and communicate her needs. Even if it initially felt strange, Emily started expressing her needs and desires. She understood that assertiveness wasn't confrontation but a way to stand up for herself while still respecting the needs of others.

Step four for Emily was to learn to set healthy boundaries and say "no" to the narcissist. Emily set healthy limits to protect her mental well-being. She realized that boundaries weren't selfish but necessary for her growth and happiness.

Emily finally decided to pursue activities she enjoyed, sought support from friends and therapists, and nurtured her mind, body, and soul.

People became aware of Emily's transformation over time. She found her voice, her strength, and her identity. As she healed, her relationship with David changed, and she decided to leave him and build a new life for herself.

Emily's story is an excellent example of the power of self-discovery and resilience. She managed to break free from codependency and emerge more robust and happier. Her journey offers hope for others trapped in similar situations, showing them they can reclaim their lives and find the love and happiness they desire.

CODEPENDENCY QUIZ

Answer the following questions honestly to determine your level of codependency in your relationship. Select a response that best portrays your thoughts and behavior. This quiz is for self-awareness and is not a substitute for professional advice.

1. Do you often put your partner's needs ahead of your own?

    a) Almost always
    b) Often
    c) Sometimes
    d) Rarely
    e) Never

2. Do you struggle to say "no" to your partner's demands?

    a) Always
    b) Often
    c) Sometimes
    d) Rarely
    e) Never

3. What is the level of your self-esteem in the relationship?

    a) Extremely low: I often feel unworthy.
    b) Low: I constantly need reassurance from my partner.
    c) Moderate: I occasionally doubt myself.
    d) High: sometimes I'm insecure.
    e) Strong: I don't rely on my partner's opinions.

4. How responsible do you feel to ensure your partner is always happy and well cared for?

a) Completely responsible
b) Mostly responsible
c) Somewhat responsible
d) Occasionally responsible
e) Not responsible at all

5. How often do you put your partner's feelings and opinions above your own?

a) Always
b) Often
c) Sometimes
d) Rarely
e) Never

6. Do you often feel anxious about your partner's reactions or moods?

a) Constantly, it's very stressful for me.
b) Often, it affects my peace of mind.
c) Sometimes, but I manage it.
d) Rarely, only on occasion.
e) Never, their emotions aren't my responsibility.

7. Would you compromise your values or beliefs to maintain the relationship?

    a) Always, even when it's against my principles.

    b) Often, I want to avoid conflict.

    c) Sometimes, if it's not a major issue.

    d) Rarely, only if it's a significant matter.

    e) Never, your values are non-negotiable.

8. How comfortable are you with spending time alone or pursuing your interests without your partner?

    a) Extremely uncomfortable, I prefer their company.

    b) Uncomfortable, but I do it occasionally.

    c) Neutral, I'm fine either way.

    d) Comfortable; I enjoy my independence.

    e) Very comfortable; I value my personal space.

9. Do you feel responsible for "fixing" your partner's problems or emotional struggles?

    a) Always; I see it as my duty.

    b) Often, I regularly take on their issues.

    c) Sometimes, depending on the situation.

    d) Rarely; I offer support but don't fix it.

    e) Never; they should manage their problems.

10. How much of your identity and happiness is tied to your partner's approval and attention?

a) Completely, I define myself through them.
b) A lot; their validation matters greatly.
c) Somewhat, I consider their opinion.
d) Slightly, it matters but not excessively.
e) Not at all; my happiness is independent.

Scoring

For questions 1, 2, 4, 5, 6, 7, 9, and 10:

a) = 5 points
b) = 4 points
c) = 3 points
d) = 2 points
e) = 1 point

For questions 3 and 8:

a) = 1 point
b) = 2 points
c) = 3 points
d) = 4 points
e) = 5 points

Interpretation

30–45 points: High Codependency

20–29 points: Moderate Codependency

10–19 points: Mild Codependency

1–9 points: Low Codependency

KEY TAKEAWAYS

- Codependents can find themselves becoming absorbed in a relationship with a narcissist.
- During the early stages of codependency, your relationship with your partner could become the most important thing in your life, and you could make sacrifices to please them. You give up something for them to the detriment of your well-being.
- During the middle stage of codependency, you could feel growing anxiety and guilt. You start to feel frustration as you realize that no matter what you do, the relationship isn't really working.
- In the late stages of codependency, emotional manipulation can affect your mental and physical health.
- If you're codependent, you usually don't have firm boundaries in your relationships. You struggle to balance giving to others and caring for your needs.
- You can take on responsibilities that aren't yours.
- You're dependent on the approval of others, which can create a never-ending cycle of wanting reassurance.

- You tend to deny your personal feelings and needs and bury your painful emotions.
- The relationship will get to a stage where you will realize that it's not possible to change the narcissist.
- You should work at becoming more assertive and practice communicating your needs.
- Assertiveness means standing up for yourself, which will help you have healthier future relationships.

In Step 3, we will look at what it takes to leave a toxic relationship.

STEP 3: BREAKING FREE – EMBRACING FREEDOM AND HEALING

A narcissist paints a picture of themselves as being the victim or innocent in all aspects. They will be offended by the truth. But what is done in the dark will come to light. Time has a way of showing people's true colors.

— KARLA GRIMES

Let's take a look at Mike's story. He had to break free from his abusive girlfriend, Charlotte, to find new meaning in his life.

I used to believe in love. That was before I met Charlotte, and our relationship left me emotionally broken. I realized too late that her beautiful smile concealed a labyrinth of manipulation and cruelty.

She captivated me at the beginning of our relationship, and we were almost excruciatingly happy. I had no idea then of the torment that awaited me in the future years of our relationship.

Initially, I found her compliments charming, but she soon started using them to manipulate my emotions. She praised me when I did what she wanted but subjected me to cold silence and temperamental mood swings when I didn't meet her expectations. I began questioning my worth and wondered why I was never good enough for her.

Charlotte started twisting reality, making me doubt my memories and perceptions of what happened in our relationship. During arguments, she manipulated my words and left me bewildered. Her gaslighting left me constantly second-guessing my thoughts and feelings.

Charlotte also removed me from my support network by isolating me from my friends and family. I tried to break free, but her grip on me became even tighter. She painted herself into victimhood, making me feel excruciatingly guilty every time she cried. I stayed with her, believing that I was the cause of her pain.

Charlotte appeared to be the perfect, caring partner to the outside world. No one knew how dark our personal life had become. I began to feel increasingly like a prisoner as my life revolved around her whims and demands.

I lost my self-esteem, and my sense of identity became increasingly unstable. My dreams and aspirations faded as her desires became the only important thing in our lives, and I continued to dance to her tune.

One day, I sat in my doctor's office when I came across an article about narcissistic abuse. I was horrified to find how accurately the descriptions matched my experiences. However, it helped me realize I wasn't alone and that there was a name for what I was experiencing.

I decided to leave her, as I couldn't see another way out. I felt uncertain and fearful, but I knew I had to break free and reclaim my sense of self for the sake of my sanity. I had to rediscover my passions, which were slowly dying.

Today, I'm married to a loving partner. However, I wanted to share my story with others who still find themselves in the same position as encouragement and a reminder that it's possible to break free from a toxic relationship and discover new meaning in the beauty of life.

HOW TO LEAVE A NARCISSIST

Leaving a relationship with a toxic and emotionally abusive person is tough, but it can be done. Knowing what to expect and how to prepare for the negativity coming your way is vital.

The best way to break up with a narcissist is to go no contact (NC), but this is also easier said than done, especially if the narcissist has played a significant role in your life. However, it's essential to cut all forms of contact. Block their phone numbers and emails to sever their access to you. It's all about protecting yourself. You're not going to be their narcissistic supply any longer.

Block them from all forms of communication, including their phone numbers. You want emails from the narcissist to end up in your junk folder, where you'll forget about them and be unlikely to see them. The narcissist will likely keep on trying to contact you. You've cut them off from you as their source of narcissistic supply, and they want that back.

Things become even more complicated when you have a child with a narcissist. If you have shared custody, you should work with a qualified therapist to compile a parenting plan. This legal document sets out boundaries about all kinds of responsibilities surrounding the children, such as time-sharing, financial obligations, or contact methods used by all the parties involved.

When you're going to break up with the narcissist, choose the safest option for you. It's best to do it as quickly as possible and not to worry about extended goodbyes. For your safety or to avoid being manipulated, you might break up through a text message or digital messaging.

Send them a straightforward message informing them that the relationship is over and wishing them the best for the future before blocking their phone number.

You need to have a plan and get everything in place before you leave the narcissist. Ensure you have physical and digital copies of your most important documents in different areas. Narcissists commonly try to control people by taking their documents, such as passports, Social Security cards, driver's licenses, and bank cards. You should even consider canceling your bank cards before you leave them, as this might be the only way to stop them from draining your bank account.

Ensure you have a secret bank account with some cash before you leave them. Start putting some money into this account as soon as possible. Narcissists are also inclined toward financial abuse, so they shouldn't know about this account and your actions. You must have access to money when you leave them.

When you leave the relationship, especially if you disappear, there is a big chance that the narcissist will try to find you. This means you must make it as difficult as possible for them to see you. The first thing you need to do is turn off the GPS on your phone.

Look at whatever other devices in your home are connected to the internet, and make sure you log out of everything.

Log out of all social media accounts and financial accounts. Delete all information that can be connected to your digital footprint.

LETTING GO OF THE PAST AND DETACHING EMOTIONALLY

If you're emotionally detached, you can observe the world around you and the people in your life without constantly being critical. This is not the same as neglecting others. It's more about understanding your place and role in life.

Emotional detachment can also help you set boundaries and let go where necessary. It will also help you base your decisions on facts, not emotional responses.

Emotions make us human, but they are also painful. Detachment from your emotions means separating yourself from them when you feel it's beneficial.

For example, without emotional detachment, an individual might accuse a loved one of not loving them during a fight. An emotionally attached person would be better able to handle strong emotions from someone else and realize that issues surrounding the relationship need to be discussed.

Emotional detachment will also make it easier for you to leave the narcissist. You're able to admit to yourself that you once loved this person. Still, they turned out to be someone different from who you were expecting, and your own emotional and physical health should end the relationship, even though this will be difficult and cause you emotional pain.

That's also why it's easier and better for your mental health to avoid contact with the narcissist when you leave them. If you allow them to contact you, they could try to "hoover" you back into the relationship. They tell you what they know you've been wanting to hear, and once they suck you back in, things will return to being the same or even worse.

If you have shared friends and connections, you should also block them. Narcissists are great at recruiting allies or flying monkeys, to their cause. They will use these people to get you back into the relationship. Surround yourself with people who support your decision to leave, and block friends or acquaintances who may try to convince you to return. Block any so-called friends who want to keep on talking about the narcissist.

Make a list of reasons why you're leaving. Looking at that list during moments of doubt or weakness could be a powerful way of reminding yourself that you're better off now. A record of what they did to you can help you stay strong when resisting their influence. It is essential to remember when they were gaslighting, lying to you, and telling you that you were misremembering things. They are good at minimizing their negative behavior and convincing you that you're overreacting.

You must permit yourself to grieve the end of your relationship with the narcissist. You now know they're monsters, but there was a time when you loved them and thought they were a different person. It's normal to feel sadness, anger, relief, and guilt. It will take you some time to deal with these emotions. Don't rush yourself.

You may have lost touch with your needs and interests during the relationship. When you're out of the relationship, you'll need some time to reconnect with who you are. Take time for self-care and to take part in activities that you enjoy.

When you want to let go of past emotional trauma, you first need to recognize that you ruminate about negative past events and that it will be better for your mental health to stop doing so. Take note of how often you experience negative thoughts. Take notice of the anger and anxiety you experience when you have upsetting memories.

You can prevent unhappy thoughts from the past from becoming stronger.

You can stop ruminating on the past by focusing on the positive. Please write down your happy memories and refer to them regularly. Don't ignore painful memories that occupy your mind; instead, replace them with one of the happy memories you've written down.

It's challenging to recover from a relationship with a narcissist, but not impossible. Reach out to your family and friends or a therapist who can provide you with support and guidance.

SETTING CLEAR INTENTIONS FOR PERSONAL GROWTH

Our intentions are our commitments, and our conscious decisions drive our actions and behavior. They go deeper than goals and objectives and reflect our beliefs, values, and desires. They guide our thoughts and emotions. We declare our purpose and direction when we set our intentions.

Our intentions will help us create the lives for ourselves that we deserve. They are the foundation and driving force behind our personal growth.

Intentions can shift our mindset and encourage us to focus on the present and the steps we're taking now rather than only focusing on the distant future.

They can also influence our personal growth in several ways:

- Setting intentions requires introspection and self-awareness. We must revisit our values and beliefs, and what is essential in our lives becomes clear. Self-reflection helps us align our aspirations with our values.
- Our intentions help us bridge the gap between our desires and actions. When we align our purposes with our values, we're more likely to make choices and take steps that align with our authentic selves.
- Our intentions can also help us when it comes to adopting a growth-oriented mindset. By focusing on the present and what we're doing today, we're changing our focus to the ongoing journey of developing ourselves and not only to a fixed outcome. The shift in mindset will help you grow your resilience and become more willing to learn from challenges.
- Intentions encourage us to understand our motivations and inner world better. It can help us see where our strengths are and where we still need to develop. Self-awareness can set personal development in motion and help us make intentional choices that encourage self-improvement.
- Intentions can also help us build resilience. When we face setbacks and challenges, our intentions remind us of the bigger picture and why we've embarked on this journey of personal growth. Strength will help us to continue working toward achieving our goals.

- They can also encourage us to change our behavior in positive ways. When we have positive intentions, we're more likely to behave in ways that support our growth.
- Our intentions can also shape our reality. When we behave by our choices and work toward achieving them, we can create a positive self-fulfilling prophecy.

How Denise Set Her Intentions for Personal Growth

Denise had recently left a relationship of some years with her narcissistic ex, and she wanted to set new goals and intentions for her personal growth.

As she took those first steps toward freedom, Denise knew that setting clear intentions for her personal growth was essential. She realized that to move forward and build a life filled with happiness and self-fulfillment, she needed a roadmap—a plan that would guide her through the ups and downs of her healing journey.

The first intention Denise set was to let go of the past. She knew that clinging to the memories of the abusive relationship would only keep her feeling pain and regret. She made a conscious decision to release the bad memories. She practiced mindfulness daily and reminded herself that her past no longer defined her.

Denise also understood that detaching emotionally from her abusive ex-partner was vital. She couldn't afford to let the narcissist continue to affect her emotions and self-esteem. She began practicing emotional detachment techniques, like visualization and affirmations, which helped her regain control over her feelings.

One of Denise's most powerful intentions was to have a clear vision for her personal growth. She reflected on what she truly wanted in life—her dreams, aspirations, and the person she wanted to become. She imagined a brighter future with each intention she set and believed she could achieve it.

Denise also realized that self-care was not a luxury but necessary for her healing journey. She prioritized self-care and incorporated activities like journaling, meditation, and exercise into her daily routine. These activities helped her to regain her inner balance.

Denise acknowledged that she didn't have to face her healing journey alone. She intended to seek support from therapists, support groups, and trusted friends. She surrounded herself with a network of people who could give her the help she needed.

Denise also celebrated her progress, even if it was small. This intention allowed her to acknowledge her resilience and appreciate the steps she was taking toward personal growth.

In the end, with each intention, she moved closer to the life of self-love and self-worth she wanted. She was optimistic about her future life, seeing endless possibilities.

ACTIVITY – WRITE A LETTER TO THE NARCISSIST

Getting away from a narcissist and starting the healing process takes courage and strength. To make things easier for yourself, you can write a letter to the narcissist, indicating the relationship is over.

You don't have to send the letter. It's more about releasing your emotions, gaining closure, and taking your power back.

You can begin your letter any way you want or use one of the examples below:

Example beginnings:

- Dear [Narcissist's name], Today, I'm writing to tell you that our relationship is over, as I want to put this painful chapter of my life behind me.
- Dear [Narcissist's name], You once held my heart captive, but I'm writing to tell you that our relationship is over today.

Examples of expressions you can use in your letter:

- I've dealt with your criticism and manipulation for too long. Today, I will finally be free.
- I will reclaim my life and build a stronger, more resilient version of myself.
- You've damaged my self-esteem, but I have vowed to care for myself and regain my confidence.

Example closings:

- Your power over my thoughts and emotions will end now. I'm taking back control of my life.
- With this letter, I close a painful chapter in my life. I deserve a happy and peaceful life.
- I have to say goodbye to you now; I will prioritize my well-being in the future.

Burn and Release Ceremony

Once you've finished writing your letter, you should have a burn and release ceremony, representing your intention of letting go of the negative emotions and energy you associate with the narcissist.

Find a space where it is safe to light the letter on fire. This could be your indoor fireplace or outside. While you watch it turn to ash, visualize how you break free from the chains holding you back.

This is a very personal process, so allow yourself to feel your emotions and treat yourself with kindness. By writing this letter, you've permitted yourself to move on to a better future.

KEY TAKEAWAYS

- When you leave a relationship with a narcissist, you must prepare as well as you can beforehand.
- The best way to break up with a narcissist is to walk away and have NC with them.

- Cut all forms of contact if you can, including blocking their phone numbers.
- The narcissist will probably keep trying to contact you, so make sure you cut all forms of digital contact with them.
- If you have a child with a narcissist and you share custody, work with a qualified therapist to create a parenting plan.
- Choose the safest option when you break up with the narcissist. Consider your safety and the possibility that you will be manipulated.
- Send the narcissist an evident and direct message that your relationship is over.
- Make sure that you have money set aside before you leave, as some narcissists are also inclined toward financial abuse.
- Emotional detachment can help you set boundaries when leaving the narcissist. It means separating yourself from your emotions when you feel this is beneficial.
- Write down why you left the narcissist and reflect on this when your resolve weakens.
- Spend some time reconnecting with who you are after you've left the relationship.

In the next step, we will examine how to reclaim your identity and build your self-worth.

STEP 4: RECLAIMING YOUR LOST IDENTITY –REDISCOVERING STRENGTH AND SELF-WORTH

If you don't like something, change it. If you can't change it, change your attitude.

— MAYA ANGELOU

This is Tom's story. He had to rebuild his self-worth after leaving his abusive girlfriend, Lucia.

If you're still in a relationship with a narcissist, I want to tell you that you're stronger than you think. Like me, you can get away from the narcissist in your life, even if you feel you don't. I emerged as a completely new person from the ashes of my former self.

I vividly remember the day I decided to leave my relationship with Lucia. It wasn't easy, as everyone had seen us as a perfect couple for a long time, and her toxicity had seeped into every corner of my life. I was a shadow of the strong and determined person I used to be. Her manipulation had stripped away my confidence, and I doubted my thoughts and feelings.

The text messages on her phone—the evidence that she had cheated on me with another man—finally made me pack my belongings. I doubted I was doing the right thing, but I also knew I deserved better. My heart pounded when I stepped out of our shared apartment, but I didn't look back.

The weeks that followed were difficult. I had broken off all contact with her, and she tried to lure me back into the relationship by any means possible. I made the mistake, at first, of staying in contact with our shared friends, but I soon learned that this was a bad idea as they became her flying monkeys as she used them against me. Anger and grief threatened to drown me, but I was determined not to let that happen. I went to therapy, which became my lifeline and helped me heal. I also learned the patterns of control and manipulation that kept me trapped for so long.

Gradually, I learned to rebuild my self-worth. I self-reflected and slowly began to piece together who I was. I reconnected with my family and friends and rediscovered old hobbies.

I gradually came out of my comfort zone and rebuilt my resilience. With the therapist's help, I realized that the daily criticism I received from Lucia was a lie and that this wasn't the person I was. Her words and actions couldn't define me but only my strength and capacity for growth. As I accepted this, my self-worth became stronger and became my guiding light into a more meaningful life.

So, while it's a difficult journey, reclaiming your self-worth is possible. Don't let the painful shadows of the past hold you back; instead, deal with them and rediscover your truth in life.

REBUILDING SELF-ESTEEM AND CONFIDENCE

It's difficult to heal from narcissistic abuse, especially if you've experienced it for a long time. That's because your self-confidence has likely been negatively influenced by what you've experienced.

You need to find out what you're good at and rediscover your strengths and talents amid the self-doubt you're experiencing. Acknowledging your abilities will help you challenge the feelings of inadequacy the narcissistic abuser may have inflicted on you.

A narcissist will affect your self-esteem, as they tend to project the painful emotions and thoughts they can't deal with themselves onto others. Inadequacy is one of the main feelings they struggle with daily.

When you find something you're good at, continue working hard and learning what you can on an ongoing basis.

It can also help your confidence a great deal if you can manage to build positive relationships. A caring support network can help you overcome the coldness and abuse you've experienced in the past.

In the aftermath of a toxic relationship, it can often feel natural to blame yourself for what happened, especially if the narcissist has projected blame onto you. They could also use their enablers or manipulate you into believing you're responsible for the abuse.

You need to set boundaries, learn to assess your needs, and say "no" to others. Saying "no" can be very liberating, as it reinforces your agency and can help you gain a newfound respect for yourself.

You may need to practice saying "no" and standing up for yourself. When you're so used to prioritizing the narcissist's thoughts and emotions over your own, you can find this difficult initially. Narcissists are highly entitled, and you might have become used to catering to their needs. For example, you might be pretty sick, but the narcissist will maintain that you're not that ill and that you can take them somewhere where they can go themselves by using public transport or walking. They could have a way of making you feel guilty until you give in to them and do whatever you can to meet their needs. This is where you would have developed the tiring habit of saying "yes" all the time to meet the needs of others. However, this behavior can only lead to exhaustion and burnout in the long term. To overcome this, you must acknowledge that you have the right to prioritize your emotions, thoughts, and feelings.

You shouldn't fear losing important people just because you say "no" to them. If you're essential to them, they will respect the boundaries you've set.

You can also build your confidence by setting challenges for yourself. When you materialize goals and challenges for yourself, you prove you have endless potential. All your accomplishments are stepping stones to rebuilding your self-esteem.

You would have had your abilities minimized and invalidated by the narcissist. They would have done this to you, as their self-esteem is fragile, while they have an unrealistic, optimistic view of themselves. They try to make up for their lack of self-esteem by acting superior and dominant over others. They will continue constantly trying to prove that they're unique and important.

If you only focus on what you can control, it will significantly help your mental health. Accept what you can't change, and by managing stress and anxiety in this way, you make it easier for yourself to build self-esteem, and it will become a habit over time.

Celebrate the successful things in your life, even if you think your victories are insignificant. Each success you have shows you the remarkable things you're capable of.

Do things that make you happy. This should all be part of your self-care routine. This will help you find a new sense of purpose in your life.

Mindfulness

This practice will help you better tune with your feelings and thoughts. By becoming more attuned to your inner self, you're opening yourself to personal growth and change. Mindfulness can help you grow in confidence and self-esteem.

It's a mental practice that means you're fully aware and present in the moment without judging yourself for your thoughts or becoming distracted by them. It can also be described as a state of conscious awareness where you focus on your feelings, thoughts, bodily sensations, and the environment around you.

So, how can you make mindfulness part of your self-esteem journey? Mindfulness can help you work on your self-esteem in the following ways:

- It can help you become more aware of your thoughts and feelings, including negative self-talk and self-critical patterns. This is the first step when it comes to changing these beliefs.
- Mindfulness also helps you observe your thoughts and emotions without immediately judging them as good or bad. This can help you be kinder to yourself and see yourself in a less harmful light.
- It can also help you to stop reacting automatically to situations or stimuli and help you respond with self-awareness to challenging situations.
- If you've suffered abuse in a toxic relationship, you may struggle to overcome rumination. Rumination involves negative thoughts playing over and over in your head.

Mindfulness can help you break this cycle of reflection by redirecting your attention to the present, which will help you end this "negative loop thinking."

- When you have a clear mind, you'll also be able to better focus on your strengths, achievements, and positive qualities, contributing to a healthier self-concept and improved self-esteem.

LETTING GO OF SELF-BLAME AND GUILT

You could be feeling a lot of guilt after ending your relationship with the narcissist. You've become so used to looking after them and catering to their needs that you may find it difficult to see how they will get along without you.

However, you must let go of feeling responsible for the narcissist. Just remember that they won't feel the same way about you or have any regard for your well-being if they end the relationship. When narcissists are done with a relationship, they usually move on quickly.

If they decide they still want you around, they will try to guilt-trip and hoover you back into the relationship, which could make you feel even worse and have the effect they desire. Just remember, if they've promised you that they will change and your relationship will be better, this isn't going to happen. Once the narcissist has got you back in their clutches, it will soon return to being just as bad again, or even worse.

If you grew up with a narcissistic parent, your feelings of guilt might be even more complicated. If you were accused of being entitled and greedy from a young age when you couldn't give your parents the validation they needed, you might fall into the trap of seeing yourself as the problem.

It's unfortunate that when you grow up with a narcissistic parent, you often tend to attract partners of the same kind.

Your inner experience from a young age might have been one of being told that you're not giving enough and that you're inconsiderate. It became natural for you to feel guilty and to try to make a narcissist happy, not to feel this terrible. Strange as this may sound, this is why you become involved in relationships with the same people. These toxic behavior methods are familiar to you, and they may even feel comfortable.

As a defenseless child, you had to keep your narcissistic abuser happy to survive; however, as an adult, you can stand alone. The narcissistic abuser's happiness no longer has to replace your own.

You could still feel selfish for putting your needs ahead of the narcissist and getting out of the relationship. It could feel like they won't be able to carry on without you, as you've been taking care of all their physical and emotional needs, just as if they were a big child.

You could also be terrified of separating from your narcissistic partner, as you think you'll spend the rest of your life alone. You might be gaslighting yourself and that your inner voice is the narcissist's bitter little voice, criticizing you with every move you make.

Embracing supportive and empathetic connections will help you overcome the guilt of leaving a narcissistic relationship. Surround yourself with supportive people who understand what you went through and can help you deal with the emotions you might be feeling, such as fear, anxiety, and guilt.

Overcoming Trauma Bonding

Forming trauma bonds is part of most dysfunctional relationships. It can be described as intense and overwhelming, also known as Stockholm syndrome or abusive bonding. People fall into the trap of this bond, as they see it as chemistry between them. However, a trauma bond is often based on familiarity, namely the bond you had with abusive childhood caretakers.

During trauma bonding, the person being abused will form a strong attachment to the abusive person. This is also a survival mechanism in response to the abuser's manipulative and inconsistent behavior.

While the trauma bond is being formed, the person can experience positive and negative interactions with the person abusing them. This can confuse you as your brain struggles to reconcile this contradictory experience. This might be easier if you have learned to equate chaos with love since childhood. You could feel loyalty and affection toward the abuser, even when they're hurting you.

How do you escape a trauma bond with a narcissist?

First, you must acknowledge the situation and what is happening to you. Admit to yourself that this is abuse. You need to be able to identify the cycles of affection and cruelty and realize that your mental health must break free from them.

It would be best to consider early childhood attachments and how this might affect your trauma bond with the narcissist. You might need help from a qualified therapist who understands narcissism and trauma bonding.

Be mindful and judge your relationship in the here and now. Consider the lies, cheating, and abuse. You have to admit to yourself that this is a toxic relationship. Look back at the intense early days of your relationship. Were there any signs then that things weren't quite as they seemed?

List the abuse you have suffered and look back on it regularly. It will remind you why you need to deal with this abuse.

The Patterns of a Trauma-Bonded Relationship

In a trauma-bonded relationship, you will also try to justify your dysfunctional partner's behavior. For example, they may have mistreated you, but you say it's because they're under stress, their cat died, or whatever else may have happened. You always discover why they're mistreating you and might not even realize you're doing this. You want to keep the relationship—at any cost. This behavior also typically starts in childhood when you might have had to justify your parents' bad behavior toward you.

Believing the lies about future behavior from the narcissist can also keep you stuck in the relationship. The narcissist may have made wonderful promises, such as that you will get married and start a family or that they will support you, but none of these ever happen. Narcissists often pull out this card when you try to leave the relationship and promise they will go to therapy and work on themselves. Don't pin your hopes on these promises. The sooner you start seeing through them, the better it will be for your mental health.

There are repetitive patterns in a trauma-bonded relationship, such as when you repeatedly have the same fight. This happens because the narcissistic partner has no intention to change. They have no empathy, and they're incapable of growth. Their personalities are rigid and don't change. You cling to the hope that things will be different, leading to repetitive fights.

You have mystical or magical thinking around your partner. Other people may point out to you that the narcissist is dysfunctional, but you continue to stay with them, as there is "something" that you can't quite point out that is compelling you to stay with them. You feel nobody understands what you see in the narcissist and why you stay with them.

You could fear leaving the narcissist, even when you realize it might be better to leave them. Confusion and fear of doing the wrong thing could cause you to stay.

Your life revolves around the narcissist, and you do everything for them. You're like a personal assistant, driver, and cheer-leader, and you even try to dress in the way they said they liked in the past. It could seem that they might eventually be happy if you continue to do everything you can to please them, but this will never really happen.

You hide your feelings and needs from the narcissist because you don't feel you can share them. It may feel like you will upset them, so you hold back and walk on eggshells around them to not set them off. You're keeping an illusion of a relationship alive.

You hide the patterns and rationalize the relationship with other people. Defending the relationship with yourself now extends to protecting it from the world at large. People tend to hide the uncomfortable parts of their toxic relationships and will be more stuck than ever.

It's important to be able to recognize these patterns. You have to acknowledge to yourself exactly why you're feeling guilty. Did you do anything wrong, or could this be because of the emotional manipulation by the narcissist? You must recognize that you're not responsible for their choices and behaviors to overcome the guilt. Regularly refer to the notes you've made about the past abuse you've suffered. Do you still feel guilty and like you should stay with the narcissist when you reflect on these dark memories?

Ultimately, you'll have to learn to forgive yourself and realize that the trauma bond was also a survival strategy. It has nothing to do with you being a bad or weak person. Be kind to yourself, learn from your errors, and let them go. It will take time to heal, and you'll have to be patient with yourself if you experience setbacks.

How Benjamin Discovered He Was in a Trauma-Bonded Relationship

Benjamin was struggling to break free from a relationship with a covert narcissist. Still, he wasn't having any success until one of his friends suggested to him that he might be in a trauma-bonded relationship. He wasn't quite sure what that meant initially, but things became more apparent when he researched and learned more about the characteristics of trauma-bonded relationships.

Benjamin realized that his relationship with his girlfriend, Daniella, was going through a repetitive cycle of abuse and then attempts at reconciliation. Daniella would be mean to him about something, and he would feel terrible about it. He didn't know how to make her happy or how to make himself feel better about what was happening. However, Daniella would suddenly be friendly to him again and apologize for her mean behavior over the past few days, stating that she had too much stress at work and would be nice to him from now on. Things would go exceedingly well for a while, and Benjamin would be pleased. However, the cycle continuously repeated itself, and Danielle treated Benjamin even worse each time than she had treated him the last time.

This rollercoaster ride of their relationship always made Benjamin feel his emotions were upheaval. He went through extreme highs and lows, from feeling love in one moment to anger and sadness in the next. He became more exhausted and confused as time went on.

He was scared of leaving the relationship, even though he knew it was ultimately toxic and harmful. Benjamin was nearing 40, afraid that time would run out for him and he wouldn't find love or acceptance elsewhere. Daniella was also a good-looking and intelligent woman, and some of his friends said he would be crazy to leave her and that he should appreciate her more. He started to think that maybe he wasn't doing enough on his side and began to cater to her needs even more.

Daniella had isolated him from many of his friends and family members, so he didn't have a strong support network on which he could rely. Benjamin found himself becoming increasingly isolated.

He downplayed Daniella's behavior, especially when she became physically abusive and threw a glass at his head. Benjamin got cut quite badly and had to go to the emergency room, but when she started crying, he told himself that she hadn't meant to hurt him and that he was probably partly to blame for her actions. He had stood up for himself, which made her angry, so she reacted.

When the physical abuse became more regular, Benjamin realized he might be addicted to Daniella. In a way, he wanted to break free from her, but at the same time, he didn't believe he could survive emotionally. He realized he was losing his identity and didn't know what he wanted from life anymore. Benjamin realized that he would have to start working on his self-confidence and self-image to end the toxic relationship and regain his life.

However, for a while, he kept holding on to the hope that she would change. When Benjamin started experiencing physical symptoms and finally had a minor heart attack, he realized he had to escape Daniella before her behavior killed him.

It was emotionally harrowing, but he exited the relationship and reclaimed his life.

HOW TO DISCOVER YOUR GIFTS AND PASSIONS

Every one of us is uniquely brilliant in our ways, but it's often easy to overlook our unique qualities and gifts. Many of us have talents that we're not even aware of. These gifts are part of who we are.

So, how do you discover your unique qualities and gifts, especially after you've been in a relationship that left you no time for yourself and your hobbies?

Discovering your unique abilities and gifts can involve a journey of self-exploration and self-awareness. You must have patience, be willing to discover your true self, and do introspection.

Embrace your curiosity and discover new things about yourself. Feel free to explore different interests and activities without fearing being judged. This could be difficult if you've been in a relationship with a judgmental narcissist for a long time.

Permit yourself to move on beyond self-doubt, and don't compare yourself with anyone else. Try things you've never done, such as picking up a paintbrush, putting on some dancing shoes, or baking a cake.

Think back to what activities you enjoyed doing as a child. Childhood passions can often show us what our natural talents are. Reconnect with hobbies you once enjoyed but possibly stopped doing because you didn't have the time or the narcissist didn't like it when you took your attention away from them.

You can also discover your gifts when you become fully absorbed in an activity and lose track of time. The state of flow is usually aligned with your natural abilities. You enjoy that activity or hobby so much that you lose track of time while doing it. For example, you take up creative writing and get lost in the characters and storylines you're creating that hours pass without noticing.

It's also good to ask your friends and family for feedback on your good qualities and gifts. They may see strengths that you're not even aware of. Maybe you've watched family members' kids, and even though you thought of it as a fun activity, they tell you that you're good with them and should possibly even consider a career working with them.

Explore new activities to learn more about yourself and your skills. It can be things you couldn't do when the narcissist was still around, such as attending evening art or baking classes. You could even discover a hidden talent or passion that could turn into a side hustle to earn extra money.

Personality Assessments

It may sound like hard work to sit down and answer many questions about yourself online, but it's ultimately worth it. After leaving a toxic relationship, you're on a journey to rediscover yourself, and these tests can reveal a lot about the inner you that you weren't even aware of.

They'll uncover different layers of your personality and help you assemble the puzzle of who you are.

So, which of these tests are worth it? There are so many out there, but knowing which ones can provide you with the best information can put you on the right track to self-discovery.

The Myers-Briggs Type Indicator (MBTI) is an excellent personality assessment tool and one of the more popular ones used today. It helps you understand how you make decisions and interact with others, which is especially useful when working on your relationships and any future relationships you may have. The MBTI can help you understand if you're an introvert or an extrovert and if you make logical or emotional decisions.

The CliftonStrengths assessment can help you understand your strengths and what you're naturally good at. You could discover that you're a natural problem solver or leader.

There's also Jordan Peterson's personality assessment, which helps you understand more about yourself and others. His questions can help you uncover your traits on various scales, such as agreeableness and extraversion.

Remember that these assessments aren't about putting you in a box or telling you who you're supposed to be; they're about giving you insight, helping you understand your natural tendencies and strengths, and discovering the areas where you need to go.

Celebrating Your Unique Strengths and Gifts

When you've just walked away from a toxic relationship, you might ask yourself why you should celebrate your strengths and gifts. Well, the fact that you've come from there to here is a testament to your resilience, and your journey isn't over yet.

During the time you spent in your dysfunctional relationship, you may have doubted your talents and gifts. Well, they're still there, waiting for you to acknowledge them. They can still light up your world; they've just been dimmed for a while.

It may feel like your toxic relationship destroyed your identity, but it doesn't have to be like that. You can regain your positive qualities, even if it takes a while.

Your toxic relationship may have left you feeling small, but you should never forget that you're still a powerful person who isn't defined by the toxic chapter in your life. Instead, you're defined by your strength to leave the relationship and heal.

Be grateful for your unique qualities and celebrate them. Your journey through life doesn't have to be defined by your toxic relationship but instead by your resilience and your ability to thrive despite all you have experienced.

ACTIVITY – IDENTIFY YOUR GIFTS AND TALENTS

Answer the following questions honestly to uncover your hidden talents and unique qualities. Your answers will help guide you on a journey of self-discovery.

1. Which of these types of activities do you enjoy doing so much that you lose track of time?

    a) Creating art or crafting
    b) Solving puzzles or coding
    c) Helping others or listening to their problems
    d) Trying new sports

2. What do people compliment you on?

    a) Your eye for detail
    b) Your problem-solving ability
    c) Your empathy and understanding
    d) Your energy and enthusiasm

3. Which of these causes interests you the most?

    a) Nature conservation
    b) Digital and technological innovation
    c) Mental health awareness
    d) Community development

4. Which of the following topics do you enjoy learning and reading about?

    a) Creative writing and literature
    b) Science and technology
    c) Psychology and human behavior
    d) Travel and different cultures

5. What do you do on your free days?

    a) Paint, draw, or create something artistic
    b) Tackle a challenging problem or project
    c) Spend time with family and friends
    d) Take part in outdoor activities, such as hiking

6. What gives you the excited butterflies feeling?

    a) Imagining your book being published and selling well
    b) Brainstorming and executing a complex project
    c) Assisting someone in need and making a positive impact
    d) Planning an adventure to an unfamiliar destination

7. Which of the following did you enjoy doing as a child?

    a) Drawing, painting, or playing a musical instrument
    b) Building structures with blocks or Legos
    c) Playing with dolls or action figures in imaginative scenarios
    d) Playing outside and climbing trees?

8. Which quality do you admire most in others?

a) Creativity and originality
b) Logical thinking and problem-solving
c) Compassion and understanding
d) Fearlessness and adventurous spirit

9. What topic could you talk about for a long time?

a) Art, design, and creative writing
b) Science, technology, or a particular subject
c) Relationships, personal growth, and emotional well-being
d) Travel experiences and cultural exploration

10. Which scenario resonates with you?

a) Painting colorful shapes onto a blank canvas
b) Using logical thinking to solve a complex puzzle
c) Providing comfort to someone in need
d) Going on an adventure to an unknown destination

Results

Count the number of times you chose each letter:

- Most A's: You're probably a more creative and expressive person.
- Most B's: Your talents are probably problem-solving and analytical thinking.

- Most C's: You have an empathetic nature, and your talent is helping others.
- Most D's: Your adventurous spirit could lead you to explore various outdoor and exploratory activities.

This quiz aims to spark your self-discovery journey. Embrace your unique qualities, nurture them, and let them guide you to a life filled with purpose and fulfillment.

KEY TAKEAWAYS

- If you've experienced narcissistic abuse for a long time, your confidence will have taken a knock.
- After leaving the relationship with a narcissist, you must rediscover your strengths and talents.
- If you acknowledge your abilities, it will help you challenge your feelings of inadequacy.
- The reason why a narcissist is so destructive to your self-esteem is because they project their painful emotions and inadequacies onto you.
- Building positive relationships will help you build your confidence.
- Being able to say "no" can help you gain a newfound sense of respect for yourself. This might not be so easy at first, especially if you struggle with self-confidence issues.
- You must acknowledge that you can prioritize your emotions, thoughts, and feelings.

- Your abilities would have been minimized and invalidated by the narcissist. They make up for their lack of self-esteem by trying to control others.
- The healthiest thing you can do is focus on what you can control in your life.
- You don't have to feel guilty after ending your relationship with the narcissist.
- Trauma bonding is one of the main things you must overcome.
- Trauma bonding can be very intense; some people experience it as chemistry; however, it's often primarily based on familiarity. If you had a bond with emotionally abusive caretakers during childhood, this type of relationship will feel natural to you.
- A trauma bond is also a type of survival mechanism in response to the abuser's manipulative behavior.
- When you want to leave a narcissist, you first have to admit that your situation is abusive. Think about lies, cheating, and other toxic behavior in the relationship.
- People in a trauma-bonded relationship often try to justify their partner's behavior.
- If you believe a narcissist's lie about the future, you will remain stuck in the relationship. This is when they make all kinds of wonderful promises, including that they will change, which never happens.
- There are repetitive toxic patterns in a trauma-bonded relationship since the narcissistic partner is incapable of changing or personal growth, and they have no empathy.

- You may feel that nobody understands what you see in the narcissist.
- You never feel like you can share your true feelings with the narcissist, and you walk on eggshells around them.
- It's vital to recognize that the narcissist is emotionally manipulating you and that the trauma bond was a survival strategy.
- You need to rediscover your strengths and abilities when you've been in a toxic relationship.
- You can now pursue your interests and activities without fearing being judged.
- Explore new activities to learn more about yourself and your skills.
- You'll discover that you still have talents and gifts, even though they may have been dimmed during your toxic relationship.

In the next step, we will explore how you can set boundaries to protect your health.

A Brief Interval

Healing is a matter of time, but it is sometimes also a matter of opportunity.

— HIPPOCRATES

There's no way of knowing how many people have experienced narcissistic abuse, but estimates suggest that over 60 million people in the US may be affected by a narcissistic relationship... as you know, it's not always easy to tell that it's happening to you.

A narcissist will make you doubt yourself. As we saw in Step 1, they may employ the hoovering technique after a bout of criticism or downplay their actions so much that you start to second guess yourself and wonder if they ever really happened.

Perhaps you picked up this book because you were unsure whether it was happening to you, or maybe you were already aware and ready to face the problem head-on. Either way, you knew you needed help – and many more people are in the same position. I want to help make the road a little easier for them, and I'd like to ask for your help. All it will take is a few moments of your time, but the difference it could make is profound.

By leaving a review of this book on Amazon, you'll show new readers where they can find the validation they're

looking for, as well as the guidance they need to break free and set themselves on the path to a happier future.

Your words will provide the signpost that new readers need to point them in the direction of the information they need to guide them out of the darkness. In essence, your words can change lives.

Thank you so much for your support. It might not feel like much, but simply by taking a few minutes to do this, you can significantly impact someone else.

STEP 5: SETTING BOUNDARIES – THE ART OF SELF-PRESERVATION AND EMOTIONAL WELL-BEING

You have to love and respect yourself enough not to let people use and abuse you. You have to set boundaries and keep them, let people clearly know how you won't tolerate being treated, and let them know how you expect to be treated.

— JEANETTE CORON

This is James's story. He avoided contact with his narcissistic girlfriend to escape her toxic influences.

I was in a relationship with a narcissist for a while, leaving me feeling like I was walking on a tightrope. The push and pull of the relationship left me feeling drained, and I felt trapped in a toxic cycle.

As time passed, I realized my manipulative partner, Lena, was destroying my happiness and that I deserved better. I still had hope for the relationship and didn't want to leave immediately, but I knew I would have to set boundaries to stay sane.

Her needs had always taken precedence, but I now realized I had to start paying attention to my own. I had to remind myself that I was also worthy of love and respect.

I started educating myself about narcissism and setting boundaries. My newfound knowledge helped me understand more about our relationship and also gave me the tools to protect myself.

I found setting boundaries daunting at first, and I had to find the courage to stand up for myself and communicate what I wasn't comfortable with. I started saying no to her unreasonable demands and reclaimed my personal space. My attempts were met with resistance and manipulation, but I remained firm.

As I learned to set boundaries, I rediscovered my interests as I had more time for myself. I prioritized activities that brought me joy and surrounded myself with uplifting people.

The relationship eventually deteriorated further, and I decided to break up and have no contact with Lena. This allowed me to heal without her toxic influence.

Setting boundaries helped me rediscover my sense of self and reclaim my life. It led me to a place of empowerment and freedom, and I now have a healthy relationship with a new partner.

After all, I had been through, I also discovered an inner strength I never knew I had.

THE IMPORTANCE OF BOUNDARIES IN RECOVERY

After you've experienced a toxic relationship, you want to reclaim your space and identity. Boundaries can help you define your space. They tell other people who you are and what you stand for.

Remember those draining conversations and manipulative mind games? Boundaries are your shield. They fend off the toxicity that once invaded your heart and soul. Recovering from narcissistic abuse means safeguarding your emotional energy. Boundaries lock the door for those who can't respect your healing journey, giving you the space to focus on nurturing yourself.

Boundaries play a crucial role because they do the following:

- Set the lines between our responsibilities and what's not on our plate.
- Spell out our comfort zones and the things that make us uneasy.
- Make it clear where our space ends and someone else's space starts.
- Express our identity, values, and the boundaries that define our limits.

Once you've stepped away from your relationship with the narcissist, you'll probably realize that there are other people in your life for whom you must also set boundaries. You may think a person is kind and has good intentions, but if their actions say something else—for example, if they're using you to do their work—you must set strong boundaries.

You may want to set the following boundaries while you recover from abuse:

Empowering Communication Boundaries

Choose how much of your personal story you want to share with others regarding your past in the toxic relationship and your journey to recovery. It's unnecessary for everyone to know what happened, as it's your personal journey and much of it is potentially also very traumatic. You can choose what to share with your support network and those closest to you. Don't just share any information online or on social media. You don't want to be judged on the traumatic experiences you went through in the past.

Narcissistic abuse silenced you and made you doubt your feelings. Boundaries permit you to express your pain and frustration. Setting boundaries sends a powerful message to yourself that your emotions matter.

Self-Care Boundaries

Make sure that you set time boundaries so that you have sufficient time for self-care. First, you need time for counseling or therapy sessions to make sure you receive support throughout the healing process. Make sure you also have enough time for other activities that can help you heal, such as exercise, yoga, or any other activity you would like to do for enjoyment.

Emotional Well-Being Boundaries

While you should educate yourself about narcissistic abuse, it's also important to realize that you may experience triggers from this education, and you need to set boundaries to prevent yourself from being overwhelmed and burning out.

Boundaries can also help you pace your recovery journey as you limit the amount of information you consume about the abuse. You don't want to trigger overwhelming emotions that can hijack your progress.

It would be best to take breaks from this to prevent emotional exhaustion. It's about putting yourself first and creating a safe and comfortable space for your recovery on your terms.

When coming out of a dysfunctional relationship, you may judge yourself harshly and tell yourself that you should have known better.

Self-compassion and self-forgiveness are essential when recovering from narcissistic abuse.

When setting boundaries with yourself, ask yourself these questions:

- How have I compromised my own needs to protect myself in the past?
- Has this strategy indeed served me well?
- How can I prioritize my well-being in the present?
- What can I do to reduce the stress in my daily life?
- How can I make time for joy and contentment?
- What do I truly need at the moment?

- What can I remove from my life that doesn't support my healing journey?

Empowering Choices and a Sense of Safety

You may feel on edge when you have to make decisions after surviving an abusive relationship. Your boundaries will help you make decisions that serve your well-being. Boundaries can help you make decisions that make you feel safe. You can create your environment and decide who gets to be part of your inner circle and who should stay out.

Creating a New Narrative

Recovery is about rebuilding your life on your terms.

It empowers you to choose the people, activities, and experiences that align with your healing and growth. Boundaries help you create a narrative where you're the protagonist, not the victim.

Boundaries help you reclaim your power, rediscover your self-worth, and nurture your healing. They're the anchors that keep you grounded as you navigate your recovery. So, embrace them as your allies; they're your roadmap to a future defined by strength and resilience.

HOW TO SET BOUNDARIES

Boundaries can create healthy bridges of understanding between you and others. You don't want to wall yourself off from other people; you simply want to control how much access they have to you.

Five different types of boundaries shape the way we connect with others and express ourselves:

1. Physical boundaries: Your physical boundary is an invisible bubble that guards your comfort zone. Maybe you like public displays of affection and kissing, but your friend enjoys her solitude and cherishes being away from a public setting.
2. Sexual boundaries: These boundaries concern your comfort with sexual comments and touches. You get to decide who enters your space or who is only allowed to admire you from afar.
3. Intellectual boundaries: You can shield your ideas and beliefs from dismissal. Your thoughts are precious, and you also have to respect the opinions of others.
4. Emotional boundaries: When you have emotional boundaries, you feel comfortable only sharing your feelings gradually with others. You will only share your emotions when you're ready to do so.
5. Financial boundaries: This is all about where your money goes and who decides how you spend it. You shouldn't feel pressured to lend money to others, especially those who have big spending habits.

Start setting boundaries by introducing a few into your life. This way of doing it gives you time to consider what suits you.

You should set your boundaries from day one in a new relationship. Whether it's a friendship or romance, let people know early on what you're okay with and what you're not.

Remember that you can always add more boundaries if you don't have enough. Sufficient boundaries at work can even enhance your performance, benefiting you financially. Why would you run around and do someone else's work while they get the promotion or raise? Boundaries will prevent you from being abused by others.

You must speak up calmly and assertively to protect your space if someone crosses the line.

In the end, you should stay balanced when setting boundaries. Trust your gut, and don't overthink. Just trust your gut and maintain a healthy balance. Let your intuition guide you.

COMMUNICATING YOUR BOUNDARIES

In the complicated world of human interaction, you must be able to set and communicate boundaries. It's your way of telling the world who you are and how you expect to be treated. However, it's not an easy skill to master, and many of us will realize, especially after leaving a toxic relationship, that we've never quite mastered it. If you grew up with narcissistic parents and had to cater to their needs from a young age, you might not even have been aware that there is such a thing as boundaries. So, let's dive into the journey of boundary setting with some practical tips.

Setting boundaries can be like starting a tricky puzzle; you might not know where to start. For example, in the past, if our needs were brushed aside and we were afraid of being seen as selfish or expected to be people-pleasers, it might even make the entire situation trickier.

Communicating your boundaries without making other people angry can be a bit of a special skill, especially if you tend to be direct. When you have low self-esteem, you may switch from passive to aggressive when you intend to be assertive while communicating boundaries. However, you can also overcome this by practicing being more assertive.

You need to be clear about what your boundaries are before communicating them. Think carefully about your needs and limits and what you're comfortable with. Identifying with them will be more straightforward when you genuinely understand your boundaries.

When expressing your boundaries, frame your statements using "I" instead of "you." Others will then be less likely to think that you're blaming or accusing them of something and will understand that you're expressing your needs and opinions. For example, say, "I need some quiet time right now," instead of "You're too noisy."

State your boundaries directly and clearly to others but respectfully and courteously. Don't be aggressive or confrontational.

Stay calm and relaxed while you're communicating your boundaries. Always keep your emotions under control, even if the situation is challenging or you think it may be getting heated. Your feelings are always valid, but you should avoid misunderstandings.

Consider the place and also the timing when you're going to communicate your boundaries. You should preferably be in a private setting to have a focused conversation. You should also choose a time when the other person and you are both calm and receptive.

After telling someone your boundaries, you should also be open to a constructive discussion. The other person may have concerns or questions. Try to be empathetic while you listen to them, and work on finding mutually acceptable solutions to challenges.

If possible, you should try to frame your boundaries in a positive light. Instead of telling them you don't want them to do something, tell them what you want them to do. Positive language could even make your boundaries feel like preferences and not restrictions.

You might have to set consequences if people ignore your boundaries. Communicating what will happen if your boundaries aren't respected is essential. This could reinforce the importance of your boundaries and may serve as a deterrent.

Once you've communicated your boundaries, listen actively to the other person's response. This will show them you value their perspective, even if you disagree. Active listening can decrease the potential for conflict and lead to more understanding.

If the other person respects your boundaries, show them you're grateful for their support. Thank them for being considerate, as positive reinforcement can strengthen your relationship.

Communicating your boundaries assertively is all about finding a balance between your needs and respecting the needs of others. It's OK if you assert yourself respectfully and are open to compromise when necessary. If you can do this, you can build relationships on mutual respect.

SETTING BOUNDARIES WITH TOXIC PEOPLE

Dealing with toxic people like narcissists can be emotionally draining and exhausting. You may have broken up with your toxic ex, but you will come across other manipulative people, such as narcissistic coworkers or family members, who cross the line and push your boundaries. You must know how to set boundaries and deal with people like these. Let's explore some practical strategies to help you do this.

It will make your life easier, and you're much less likely to be manipulated if you set boundaries for the toxic people in your life. The first thing you need to do is be aware of your limits. How do you feel after interacting with this type of person? Are they constantly crossing your boundaries? If you're uncomfortable after dealing with them, it's a clear sign that you must immediately take action and set boundaries. Decide if it's in your best interest to interact with them at all. If you take a break from them, you should be able to regroup and reassess your boundaries.

It's essential to communicate your boundaries assertively when you're dealing with toxic people. Be explicit about what you need them to do and your expectations of them. You should prioritize your well-being and never feel bad about it. Remember that they always prioritize their wants and needs, and they don't actually care about yours or how you think.

Hold narcissists responsible for their behavior, and don't make excuses for them. Narcissists are often great at making excuses for themselves, and they're good at dodging accountability and responsibility. There are always traumatic childhoods, negative past experiences, and other people who are responsible for their behavior. They will try to guilt-trip you into believing this.

If boundaries aren't working for you in a relationship with a toxic person, you need to be prepared to walk away from them. Cutting off all contact is often your best option when dealing with narcissists.

How Helena Set Boundaries With the Toxic People in Her Life

Helena had always been a kind and compassionate person. She had a heart that seemed to have no limits, and she often went out of her way to help others. While her empathy was a beautiful trait, it also made her susceptible to being taken advantage of by the toxic people in her life.

One day, after a particularly draining encounter with her manipulative coworker, Mark, Helena realized that she had to do something. She couldn't continue allowing toxic people to walk all over her and drain her energy. She decided it was time to set boundaries.

Helena began her journey by taking a moment to reflect on her needs and limits. She asked herself which behaviors and interactions were causing her distress and which were crossing the line. This self-reflection helped her see in which areas of her life she needed to set boundaries.

Next, Helena thought about the people in her life causing her the most stress and discomfort. She recognized that Mark at work was a good example, but other friends constantly took but never gave, and even some family members pushed her emotional buttons.

With a better understanding of her own needs and the toxic relationships in her life, Helena was ready to communicate her boundaries to the people in her life. She knew this would not be easy, but she was determined. She started with Mark at work.

One afternoon, she asked him for a private conversation. With kindness but firmness, she explained that she couldn't tolerate his constant criticism and attempts to take credit for her work. She told him that she expected mutual respect and cooperation. She was surprised when Mark seemed taken aback but agreed to a more respectful work dynamic.

Helena continued her boundary-setting journey with her friends and family. She began to say "no" when she felt over-whelmed or their requests crossed her limits. She initially found it difficult, as she worried about disappointing people, but she reminded herself that her well-being mattered too.

She found that some people respected her boundaries while others pushed back. She was prepared for this and had already decided what she would do. For those who continued to ignore her limits, she distanced herself or, in some cases, ended the relationship.

Helena's friends and therapist supported her with her boundary-setting and provided her with guidance, encouragement, and a sense of community during the challenging times she experienced.

Her life gradually got better. She no longer felt drained and overwhelmed by toxic people. Instead, she surrounded herself with those who respected her boundaries and appreciated her for who she was. Helena had learned that setting boundaries was an act of self-respect and self-love, allowing her to reclaim her life, energy, and happiness.

KEEPING A JOURNAL

Keeping a journal can help you a great deal when you're recovering from a toxic relationship. It encourages you to see yourself differently and change your mindset about potential future relationships.

Journaling provides a safe, private space to express the feelings you may have hidden in your toxic relationship. Writing down your feelings and thoughts will help you release pent-up emotions.

It's also easier to understand the dynamics of your relationship if you can write them down on paper and refer back to them.

You may start to notice patterns, which can help you understand how this relationship impacts your mental and physical health. It will hopefully also help you see what you can do to avoid becoming involved in such relationships.

Your journal can also help you when it comes to setting boundaries. Suppose you see your experiences written down, your values, and what is important to you. In that case, it can help you consider future relationships and avoid similar toxic dynamics.

Writing in your journal can also help you keep track of your healing and recovery from your toxic relationship. You can reread earlier entries to see how your mindset and perspective have changed. It can also remind you of how resilient and strong you are and help you regain your confidence after the end of your destructive relationship.

You can also use your journaling activity to set goals after leaving your relationship. Also, consider setting goals for your future relationships. When you write down goals, they will also feel more achievable.

Journaling can help shift your focus to the things that are working in your life and could help you develop a more positive outlook.

Finally, journaling can also give you closure after you leave your relationship. You could even write a letter to your former partner expressing your feelings.

Let's move on to a journal activity that can help you when it comes to setting boundaries.

JOURNAL ACTIVITY – SELF-REFLECTION AND SETTING BOUNDARIES

This worksheet will help you identify and communicate your boundaries effectively, which will help you not become involved in toxic relationships. Think carefully about the answers and write them down in your journal.

- Let's identify your boundaries. Are there any areas of your life in which you feel your boundaries are being violated? This could be in your personal or professional life. Write down what exactly it is that's rubbing you the wrong way.
- Clarify some boundaries for the behavior that bothers you. Use "I" statements to express your boundaries; for example, "I need ..."
- Identify with whom you need to communicate boundaries. How will you share it with them, and when? Write down some ideas on what you will say, and be as respectful as possible.
- Write down some consequences of what will happen if someone continues to violate your boundaries. This could include reducing or ending contact.
- Review your progress regularly when it comes to reviewing your boundaries. Have you been able to maintain them? What have you learned?

KEY TAKEAWAYS

- Boundaries are essential when you're recovering from a toxic relationship.
- Boundaries can protect you against manipulation and are a way of safeguarding your emotional energy.
- By setting boundaries, you're telling yourself that your emotions matter.
- Your boundaries will help you when it comes to making decisions about your well-being.
- Boundaries can also help you create a narrative where you're the hero in your own life and not a victim.
- Boundaries can help you rediscover your self-worth.
- Five different boundaries shape how we connect and interact with others.
- You need to set your boundaries assertively without making others angry.
- Try to frame your boundaries in a positive light, as it might get a better reaction from the other person.
- Hold narcissists responsible for their behavior, and don't make excuses.

In the next chapter, we will look at how you can deal with the challenges of recovery.

STEP 6: OVERCOMING THE CHALLENGES OF RECOVERY – RISING FROM THE ASHES

Half the harm done in this world is due to people who want to feel important. They don't mean to harm, but the harm [that they cause] does not interest them. Or they do not see it or justify it because they are absorbed in the endless struggle to think well of themselves.

— T. S. ELIOT

This is Sylvia's story. She recovered from the PTSD she suffered after her relationship with a narcissist with the help of a therapist.

I went through a deeply traumatic experience with narcissistic abuse and recovering from PTSD with the help of a therapist. I decided to share my story in the hope that it could help others with their recovery process.

I carried the weight of narcissistic abuse with me for many years, unaware of its toll on my mental and physical health. I only went to a therapist when I couldn't take it.

My first session with the therapist was simply nerve-wracking. I was hopeful, but I also felt a large amount of fear. I still remember it vividly. I felt a mixture of fear and hope, and it was a relief to have a safe space to express my emotions finally.

My therapist guided me patiently and empathetically through the process.

We discussed the link between narcissistic abuse and post-traumatic stress disorder (PTSD). It was a revelation to understand that the constant manipulation, gaslighting, and emotional turmoil I had endured had left me with symptoms of PTSD. It was a relief to know that I wasn't going crazy.

The therapist helped me unravel my emotions, listened as I poured out my experiences, and validated my feelings, helping me understand how the abuse had affected my self-worth.

One of the most valuable aspects of therapy was learning grounding exercises to manage anxiety. I had spent years feeling like I was walking on eggshells, and anxiety had become my constant companion. I regained control over my racing thoughts and panic attacks through mindfulness and deep breathing exercises. These exercises helped me reconnect with the present and find a sense of calm amidst the chaos in my mind.

Journaling became my lifeline in the healing process. The therapist encouraged me to pour my thoughts onto the pages of a journal. I found it freeing to express myself in this way. Journaling also felt like a safe space for self-reflection and building self-awareness. It allowed me to track my progress, identify triggers, and set goals for my recovery.

With each therapy session, I started to feel more in touch with myself, as if I were reclaiming parts of my personality that I thought had been lost forever. It was a challenging journey that helped me transform my life. I have to say that the therapist's support and guidance were instrumental in my recovery.

I hope my story will help you start your journey to recovery.

COMPLEX POST-TRAUMATIC STRESS DISORDER (CPTSD)

Understanding complex post-traumatic stress disorder (CPTSD) is about acknowledging the significant emotional and psychological toll these experiences can have on people.

CPTSD is a condition that is becoming increasingly recognized, especially in the context of narcissistic abuse.

It's important to note that while CPTSD is not officially classified as a diagnosis in the DSM-5 (the American Psychiatric Diagnostic Manual), it is acknowledged in the ICD-11 (the International Classification of Diseases).

CPTS differs somewhat from general PTSD because it originates in ongoing, recurring trauma. For example, when it comes to narcissistic abuse, it involves the manipulation suffered in a relationship with someone who displays narcissistic traits. If you're the victim of a narcissist, you may have suffered emotional, psychological, and possibly physical abuse over an extended period.

The Signs of CPTSD

It's complicated and painful to live with CPTSD, which can result from narcissistic abuse.

Frequent flashbacks are one of the most harrowing symptoms of CPTSD. You could be haunted by flashbacks that cause you to relive traumatic memories from your past. Your painful memories are like ghosts that never seem to rest. These memories take on their own life and rear their heads when you least expect it. These flashbacks could make it difficult to focus and enjoy living your life in the present moment.

You could develop constant hypervigilance as a survival mechanism. Imagine you're living in a world where it feels to you like danger is everywhere. Even when you know you should feel safe, you're scared of being attacked at any moment. You're always on high alert and looking out for threats. This will exhaust you long-term because you feel like you're on a battlefield with an elusive enemy, always surrounded by fear.

You can experience a rollercoaster of shame, fear, sadness, and anger. You may feel as if you're trapped in a storm and there's no shelter available. The turmoil could be so overwhelming that you even find it challenging to navigate your daily life. It's difficult to find stability on such shaky ground.

Relationships form the foundation of human connection, but if you're dealing with CPTSD, they could become a maze that is increasingly difficult to navigate. Narcissistic abuse could have destroyed your ability to trust, as you might fear that you'll be hurt again. Difficulty trusting others can cause strained relationships with friends, family, or romantic partners. It might feel like you're trying to build a bridge over a deep chasm, and trust is the missing part.

Overcoming CPTSD

CPTSD can't be conquered overnight and can be quite a journey to recovery. However, it's possible with proper support, such as a trained trauma professional.

Different forms of therapy, like psychotherapy, somatic therapy, and eye movement desensitization and reprocessing (EMDR), can also help you significantly heal from narcissistic abuse.

Psychotherapy

Cognitive-behavioral therapy (CBT) is used to treat CPTSD. It can help you recognize and challenge the negative beliefs and thought patterns you may have developed due to the abuse. The aim is to create healthier ways of thinking.

Dialectical-behavior therapy (DBT) can help you if you're struggling with emotional regulation difficulties, which are common in CPTSD. It teaches mindfulness and emotional regulation.

Traditional talk therapy gives you a safe space to discuss your experiences and feelings. When you can express your emotions, you'll also be able to deal with your trauma and learn more about your behaviors and thought patterns.

Somatic Therapy

Somatic therapy considers the trauma that is stored in your body. This approach combines talk therapy with body-centered techniques to help you release physical tension and stored trauma. It can include the following techniques:

- Body scanning involves guiding clients to pay attention to physical sensations and body tension. This can help them identify areas in their bodies where tension is held, allowing for release and relaxation.
- Somatic therapy often involves various breathing exercises that can help you regulate the nervous system and reduce the physiological effects of trauma, such as hypervigilance.

You can do gentle exercises that will make you more aware of your body and help you reconnect with your physical self safely and in a controlled way.

Eye Movement Desensitization and Reprocessing (EMDR)

EMDR is a specialized therapeutic technique that will help you deal with the memories of the trauma you experienced.

It works in the following ways:

- The therapist will first assess your trauma history and identify specific target memories or distressing events that must be addressed.
- You will take part in bilateral stimulation during the therapy session. This can involve tracking the therapist's moving finger with your eyes, listening to alternating sounds, or feeling gentle taps on your hands. It can help you reprocess your memories of the trauma.
- During bilateral stimulation, you will deal with your memories safely and carefully. The idea is that this should help you reevaluate and reintegrate your memories, making them less powerful and helping you feel emotionally less distressed.

How Justine Overcame CPTSD

Justine was resilient and had survived a tumultuous, emotionally scarring relationship with a narcissist. Although she had left her partner, the scars of complex post-traumatic stress disorder (CPTSD) still haunted her daily.

The memories of the relentless emotional abuse, manipulation, and gaslighting made it difficult for her to find peace within herself. She had nightmares, and during the day, she was tortured by flashbacks.

Justine was determined to regain control over her life and overcome the emotional torment. She had heard about eye movement desensitization and reprocessing (EMDR), a therapeutic technique known for its effectiveness in treating trauma, and decided to try it.

Justine knew that she would need the help of a trained therapist. She contacted Dr. Stevens, a compassionate and experienced EMDR therapist in her town. Dr. Stevens provided her with a supportive environment for her healing journey.

In her therapy sessions, Justine explored her traumatic memories and the emotions they stirred. She recounted the moments of abuse, the feelings of helplessness, and the constant anxiety she'd felt for so long. Dr. Stevens encouraged her to go deep into these painful memories.

Justine's memories would resurface during the EMDR sessions, and she would work through them with Dr. Stevens' support. As her eyes followed a moving light or the therapist's hand, she found that the memories had lost some emotional charge. Over time, the nightmares began to subside, and she felt less traumatized.

Through EMDR and therapeutic discussions, she began challenging the negative beliefs her narcissistic ex-partner instilled.

Justine experienced changes in her emotional well-being as she continued the therapy sessions. The traumatic memories that once held her captive no longer had the same power over her. She found peace within herself and a sense of closure regarding her past.

Justine's EMDR journey had transformed her life. The trauma of her past relationship no longer defined her, and she had increased her resilience.

GROUNDING TECHNIQUES THAT WILL HELP YOU COPE WITH ANXIETY

Dealing with anxiety can be incredibly challenging, especially after experiencing narcissistic abuse. But remember, you're not alone, and there are grounding techniques that can help you find peace and balance. Let's explore these techniques in an empathetic way.

Deep Breathing

Deep breathing can feel like a calming sea washing over you when your anxiety levels increase.

Here's how to do it:

- Lie or sit down in a comfortable place.
- Close your eyes and breathe slowly through your nose for four counts.
- Fill your lungs with air.
- Hold your breath for another count of four. Let that soothing breath linger within you.
- Exhale gently and completely through your mouth for a count of four. Imagine releasing tension and worry with each breath.
- Repeat this process a few times. Focus on the rhythm of your breath.

- Deep breathing helps slow your heart rate, calm your mind, and bring you back to the present moment, making it easier to cope with anxiety.

Moving Your Body

Physical movement can be a lifeline when anxiety makes you feel restless and agitated.

Here's what you can do:

- Engage in some form of exercise, like going for a brisk walk, a jog, or even a workout session at the gym. Moving your body helps release built-up tension and anxiety.
- Dancing is another fantastic way to release excess anxious energy. Put on your favorite music and let yourself dance freely. Don't worry about looking graceful; it's about expressing yourself and feeling the rhythm.
- Moving your body not only burns off anxious energy but also boosts the release of feel-good chemicals in your brain, like endorphins, which can help improve your mood.

Yoga Poses

Yoga can be a gentle, grounding practice connecting your mind and body.

Lie on your back with your arms stretched at your sides. Your knees should be bent, and you must bring them up to your chest. Your shoulders should be on the ground while you lower your knees to one side. Take a few deep breaths and switch to the other side.

Sit close to a wall and swing your legs up to rest against it while your back remains on the floor. This pose will help you feel calmer.

Remember, these grounding techniques help you cope with anxiety after narcissistic abuse. It's okay to take things one step at a time and seek support from friends, family, or a mental health professional when needed. You deserve to find peace and healing on your journey to recovery.

THE HEALING POWER OF JOURNALING

It takes immense courage to embark on a healing path after surviving narcissistic abuse. This journey has its ups and downs, but journaling is a powerful tool to support you.

Journaling is like having a safe haven for your thoughts and emotions, where you can be your most authentic self. It's personal and private, just for you. When you put pen to paper (or fingers to keyboard), you give a voice to your feelings, fears, and hopes.

Allow yourself to write freely and explore all your emotions around your recovery. This can help you feel released and provide you with a sense of relief.

Journaling can be your companion on the path to under-standing abusive relationships. Write about your experiences, the red flags you may have missed, and how you felt during those moments. This can help you gain a better understanding of what happened and help you make better choices in the future.

Through emotional and autobiographical journaling, you can trace your journey of personal growth. Think about your progress, even if it feels small. Celebrate your victories, as they are stepping stones to rebuilding your self-esteem.

Sharing your story about surviving narcissistic abuse can also help others on their journey. By sharing your experiences and how you've overcome challenges, you offer hope and guidance to those facing similar struggles.

ACTIVITY – JOURNAL PROMPTS

Journal prompts can help you explore your emotions, thoughts, and experiences. Choose some of the following prompts and write as much as possible in your journal.

Think about your relationship.

- What first attracted you to the person who abused you?
- How did you feel during the early stages of the relationship?
- Were there any early warning signs of abuse that you might have missed?

Understand the abuse.

- Describe the types of abuse you experienced (emotional, verbal, and physical).
- How did the abuse make you feel about yourself and your worth?
- Did you ever rationalize or justify the abuser's behavior? Why?

Rebuild your self-esteem.

- List three positive qualities about yourself that you want to embrace.
- How can you practice self-compassion and self-care every day?
- Write a letter to your past self, offering yourself encouragement and love.

Set boundaries.

- What boundaries do you need to set to protect yourself from future harm?
- How can you assertively communicate your boundaries to others that don't offend them?
- Describe a situation where you successfully set and enforced a healthy boundary.

Grieve the relationship.

- What aspects of the relationship are you mourning the most?
- How has the abuse affected your trust in others?
- What steps can you take to help yourself heal?

Reclaim your power.

- Write about a moment when you felt empowered or in control of your life.
- List five things you're proud of accomplishing despite your challenges.
- How can you continue to assert your independence and autonomy?

Participate in self-care and healing activities.

- Describe a self-care routine that brings you comfort and peace.
- What activities or hobbies make you feel genuinely happy and fulfilled?
- Write about when a healing activity helped you cope with emotional pain.

Forgive and let go.

- Reflect on your feelings toward the abuser. Do you feel angry and resent them?

- How can you release any negative emotions holding you back from healing?
- Write a letter to the abuser (without intending to send it) expressing and releasing your feelings.

Find support and self-compassion.

- List three people in your life who offer you support and understanding.
- How can you practice self-compassion and self-forgiveness during your healing journey?
- Describe a time when you felt genuinely supported by someone you trust.

Look ahead.

- What are your hopes and dreams for the future?
- What can you do to get closer to achieving your goals?

KEY TAKEAWAYS

- Complex post-traumatic stress disorder (CPTSD) is usually the result of trauma experienced more than once.
- People suffering from CPTSD relive their awful experiences through frequent flashbacks.
- Since CPTSD sufferers develop hypervigilance as a survival mechanism, you could expect danger to lurk everywhere around you and always be on high alert.

- Deep breathing exercises can help you deal with anxiety.
- Journaling has a healing power, as it will help you express and process your emotions. You can also trace your personal growth through your journaling.

The next chapter will examine how you can thrive in new relationships after recovery.

STEP 7: EMBRACE NEW RELATIONSHIPS – THRIVE AND PROSPER

I tell adults I work with never to waste their time arguing with a narcissist. You cannot win with a narcissist. Their perspective is always theirs.

— DEEDEE CUMMINGS, M.ED., LPCC, JD

This is Lisa's story. She started a successful new relationship after recovering from her relationship with a narcissist.

I was in a toxic, narcissistic relationship that stripped me of my self-worth. The emotional rollercoaster, manipulation, and gaslighting had left me shattered. At that time, I never thought this was the first step of my journey to recovery and a new, healthy relationship.

While healing with the help of a therapist, I slowly rediscovered the person I used to be. My joy and passion for life slowly came back as I rekindled my passions. I found myself becoming stronger as I cultivated my self-love and self-compassion.

I unexpectedly met someone new. This wasn't my plan, but the person was patient and kind and loved me for who I was.

I was initially scared since my past taught me to be careful about others. However, my new relationship was built on respect and empathy. They encouraged me to share my emotions and listened without judging me.

My fear improved with time. I allowed myself to be vulnerable again and to open up to my new partner about my past. Fortunately, they didn't run away or dismiss my feelings but offered me support and understanding.

As time passed, I realized I was finally in a healthy relationship. There was no manipulation or cruelty but trust and genuine care. It felt as if I could finally breathe after years of suffocating.

The new relationship was also about finding myself again, and I realized I deserved respect and kindness. I was capable of love despite my past.

NINE TRUTHS TO EMBRACE: A RECAP

Navigating life after surviving abuse is a journey filled with challenges and triumphs. You need some truths to guide you and illuminate the path toward healing, self-compassion, and the possibility of healthier relationships.

So, let's take a look at these truths:

1. You can't be blamed for how the abuser behaved or what they did to you. You were a victim, not a collaborator. You're still a worthy person after the abuse you suffered.
2. Love won't change your abuser. It's natural to think that your love can transform someone. Remember that the abuser's behavior results from their pathology, and you can do nothing about it. You're not responsible for fixing them.
3. You deserve to be part of a healthy relationship. You are worthy of respect, safety, and love without conditions. Your past experiences do not define your worthiness. You have the right to have relationships that are best for your well-being.
4. It may seem like your healing is full of ups and downs, but it's possible, and there's hope for a better life. With the proper support, you can find peace and happiness beyond abuse.
5. You don't have to justify leaving the narcissist. Leaving a relationship like this is an act of courage and strength. You've made a valid decision when you decided to put

your safety and well-being first, and you don't have to justify it.

6. Forgive yourself and treat yourself with kindness, which will help you move forward. Forgive yourself for your shortcomings, as you would forgive one of your friends.

7. Never think of yourself as being the crazy one. Gaslighting and manipulation can confuse anyone and leave you doubting your sanity. Accept your reality as valid and trust your instincts and experiences.

8. You deserve to be treated better. It's perfectly possible to have a healthy relationship. You must recognize your worth and connect with others who honor your well-being and boundaries.

9. Think of your journey as a learning experience and as not being in vain. Use the knowledge gained from your experiences to set stronger boundaries, protect yourself, and support others facing similar challenges. Your resilience can be a beacon of hope for others.

FORGIVENESS

Forgiveness involves releasing negative emotions such as anger or a desire for revenge toward someone who hurt you.

It is an act of self-healing and being compassionate to yourself as you consciously decide to let go of the emotional burden that you associate with the hurtful actions of the other person. The focus is your well-being; you don't have to reconcile with the person who harmed you.

Why Forgiveness Is Important

Forgiveness isn't easy, but it's often the healthiest way forward. It frees us from the past, elevates our mood, and makes it easier to deal with destructive emotions like anger, anxiety, and depression. In the long term, it helps us to become more optimistic and liberates us from our negative feelings.

Forgiveness is also empowering, especially when reconnecting to our authentic selves after leaving a toxic relationship. It shifts our focus to becoming survivors and shows us we can choose how to react in hurtful situations. It can also free us from grudges and unforgiveness holding us down. It can be liberating to put something down and move forward unencumbered.

Letting go of grudges can also have significant health benefits, such as less anxiety, fewer symptoms of depression, lower blood pressure, better heart health, and a stronger immune system. Overall, you'll also have better mental health and self-esteem.

Forgiving yourself for becoming involved in a relationship with a narcissist can be difficult, especially since it's so psychologically draining, but it's an integral part of the healing process.

You should acknowledge and validate your feelings and understand that it's normal to feel a range of emotions when you come out of this type of relationship. Allow yourself to handle all your emotions without judging yourself.

Learn as much as possible about narcissistic personality disorder and how narcissists manipulate and control others.

This can also help you appreciate that these relationships are complex and that what happened isn't your fault.

Treat yourself with kindness and focus on your healing through self-care and doing things that bring you joy.

Finally, let go of any shame you may feel because you became the victim of a manipulator. It's important to realize that forgiving yourself will take time. You can start by forgiving yourself for not recognizing who and what your partner was earlier.

EMBRACE THE POTENTIAL OF NEW RELATIONSHIPS

Starting a new relationship after surviving narcissistic abuse might feel like uncharted territory. It's daunting but exhilarating. You have a new lease on life and another chance to find happiness.

It's essential to be attuned to potential red flags when you start a new relationship. Having survived narcissistic abuse, you may have developed a heightened sensitivity to signs of manipulative behavior. Setting boundaries is your way of safeguarding your newfound sense of self.

It's normal to have trust issues and other insecurities due to your past experiences. It's courageous to acknowledge this. You're declaring that you refuse to let your past define your future.

Setting boundaries is a profound act of self-care. It's saying you won't allow others to mistreat you again. They protect your heart and should remind you of your worth and that you deserve dignity.

Reducing contact with your narcissistic ex goes hand in hand with reclaiming your life. You're declaring yourself independent from their toxic influence. This allows you to regain control over your emotions and decisions and reminds you that you can write your own story.

Not reacting to a narcissist is challenging, but it will empower you. It will show them you control your emotions and maintain your composure. Be prepared for a backlash because it will anger the narcissist if you refuse to participate in their mind games.

Share your past experiences with your new partner, as this will allow them to understand your journey better. You tell them you trust them enough to share your journey with them. Honesty will help you gain trust and empathy in your relationship.

Your recovery journey is also about personal growth. It's about rebuilding self-esteem, nurturing self-worth, and committing to healthier relationships. Every step you take shows your resilience and strength.

Find professional help if you feel that you need it. They will offer you guidance, resources, and validation. It's a way of saying you're worthy of healing and will invest in your well-being.

Don't be in a hurry to rush into a new relationship. Perhaps one of the most vital truths is that healing takes time. You shouldn't rush into a new relationship, as you can end up with more emotional damage. It's an acknowledgment that you are willing to be patient with yourself, allowing yourself to heal, grow, and be ready for a healthy connection when the time is right.

WHAT DOES A HEALTHY RELATIONSHIP LOOK LIKE?

A healthy relationship is like a sanctuary of love, trust, and understanding where two people come together to create a bond that nurtures their growth and happiness. Each partner respects the other's boundaries in a healthy relationship and celebrates the other partner's individuality.

The partnership is built on mutual support, where affection flows freely, and conflicts are resolved with respect and empathy.

Trust plays a vital role in healthy relationships. It's like a sturdy foundation that supports emotional intimacy and reliability. In a healthy relationship, you can rely on your partner because you know they have your best interests at heart.

Honest and respectful communication is the lifeline of a healthy relationship. It would help if you shared your thoughts, fears, and dreams without the fear of judgment. Communication enables you to connect with others and understand them.

Patience can guide us through challenging moments. In a healthy relationship, you find understanding and support.

A strong relationship always has two empathetic partners. Empathy helps you see the world through someone else's eyes.

It's about understanding each other's perspectives and offering support, even during dark times.

Affectionate gestures and genuine interest in each other's lives are daily reminders of love. They reaffirm your connection and keep the flame of passion alive.

The partners in a flexible relationship are usually also flexible. Flexibility is the ability to make compromises and be adaptable. It's about adjusting to day-to-day life and decision-making and ensuring you and your partner feel valued.

Expressing gratitude is a way of saying that you appreciate your partner. You'll acknowledge and enjoy each other's contributions in a healthy relationship.

Healthy relationships always have space for both partners to grow and to support each other's journeys of self-discovery.

Respect is about treating each other with dignity, valuing opinions, and safeguarding privacy. It's the recognition that every individual's voice matters.

Healthy relationships also thrive on give-and-take. It's about sharing responsibilities, joys, and sorrows without keeping score. It's the understanding that both partners contribute to the relationship's well-being.

Disagreements are a part of any relationship, but in a healthy one, they are handled with respect and empathy. It's about finding common ground and nurturing your connection, even when differences arise.

In a healthy relationship, individuality is celebrated, and boundaries are respected. You are unique people with your dreams and goals.

Consent is an unequivocal agreement between partners for any sexual activity. It's about continuously checking in with your partner to ensure everyone is comfortable and willing. Silence or lack of resistance does not count as consent.

JOURNALING ACTIVITY – HEALTHY RELATIONSHIPS

This journaling activity provides a safe way to reflect on your past experiences and determine what you want from future ones.

Find somewhere where you won't be disturbed. Play some soothing music or do something else that makes you feel relaxed. Then start doing the following writing exercises:

- Write down your emotions and how you feel at this moment. It's okay to feel mixed emotions—anger, sadness, relief, and confusion. Just let your feelings flow, and don't judge them.
- List three things you're grateful for today. Then, write a message acknowledging how strong and resilient you were to leave the abusive relationship.
- Write about your journey, from when you left your relationship to where you are today. Share information about what you've learned.

- Make a list of qualities and behaviors that you believe are essential to a healthy relationship. Define why these qualities are important to you.
- Reflect on the boundaries you want to establish in future relationships and write them down.
- Imagine yourself in a healthy relationship. Describe what it looks and feels like. What kind of partner do you see yourself with? How do you communicate and support each other?

KEY TAKEAWAYS

- It can be challenging to create a new life after leaving an abusive situation.
- Realizing certain truths about your abusive situation, such as that you weren't responsible for your abuser's actions and that you're still worthy, will help you heal.
- The abuser's behavior is because of their pathology, and you can do nothing about it.
- You might think your love can help the abuser, but they won't change, and you're not responsible for fixing them.
- You are worthy of respect and love. You deserve a healthy relationship. Your past experiences don't define your worthiness.
- Leaving a narcissist is an act of courage that doesn't have to be justified.

- Forgive yourself and treat yourself with kindness like you would treat one of your friends who had suffered abuse.
- You might find it daunting to start new relationships after surviving narcissistic abuse, but see it as a second chance for happiness.
- Set boundaries and look for red flags when starting a new relationship.
- Setting boundaries is self-care, indicating to others that you won't allow anyone to mistreat you again.
- It's challenging not to react to a narcissist, but it will empower you by showing them that you control your emotions. It will anger them if you aren't prepared to participate in their mind games.
- Share your past experiences with your new partner.
- A healthy relationship has space for both partners to grow as people.
- Disagreements are handled with respect and empathy in a healthy relationship.

BONUS STEP 8: PROTECTING YOURSELF FROM YOUR EX

Stay away from lazy parasites who perch on you just to satisfy their needs; they do not come to alleviate your burdens. Hence, their mission is to distract, detract, extract, and make you live in abject poverty.

— MICHAEL BASSEY JOHNSON

Sarah had been through a challenging time dealing with her narcissistic ex-partner, Max. Sarah and Max had once been deeply in love; they had two beautiful children together. However, Max's narcissistic traits began to surface as time passed, causing turmoil in their relationship.

Max was charismatic and charming but also manipulative, self-centered, and emotionally abusive. Sarah had often felt like she was walking on eggshells, trying to avoid setting off his explosive temper. Despite their separation, they still had to co-parent their children, which made her life a constant struggle.

Max tried to control and manipulate Sarah in the early days of the separation. He belittled her parenting choices, criticized her decisions, and used the children as pawns in their power struggle. It was emotionally exhausting, and Sarah often felt overwhelmed and defeated.

Sarah didn't give up easily. She knew her children's well-being was at stake and wanted to create a safe and loving environment. Sarah sought help and support from therapists and support groups, and she learned strategies to cope with co-parenting a narcissist.

One of the first things Sarah realized was that she had to set clear boundaries with Max. She established a strict communication plan, communicating with him only through email or a co-parenting app to minimize direct contact and emotional manipulation. This helped reduce the toxicity in their interactions and provided a documented record of communication.

Sarah also focused on her emotional well-being. She practiced self-care diligently, made time for enjoyable activities, and looked after her mental health. She learned to recognize the signs of emotional manipulation and detachment, which allowed her to maintain her composure during challenging interactions.

As time passed, Sarah's patience and persistence began to pay off. Max's attempts to control her and manipulate the children became less frequent and less effective. Sarah's consistent approach to co-parenting and commitment to her children's welfare created a more stable and secure environment.

Through therapy, Sarah also learned to talk to her children about narcissism and toxic behavior. She helped Emma and Jake understand that their father's actions were not their fault and taught them coping strategies to deal with difficult situations.

Sarah still faces challenges occasionally, but her commitment to her children's happiness and well-being helps her get through this.

STRATEGIES TO PROTECT YOURSELF AFTER THE BREAKUP

Breakups can be challenging, and when you've been in a relationship with someone who exhibited narcissistic traits, the aftermath can be especially tough. You can follow some strategies to protect yourself and maintain your well-being.

Accept that it's doubtful that your ex is going to change. They won't suddenly gain insight or take responsibility for their actions. They will still find a way to blame you for everything, including the breakup. Be careful of them hoovering you back into the relationship, as this will be a time when you could be especially vulnerable to this behavior.

Your first step in moving forward is acknowledging and accepting that the relationship has ended. Your narcissistic ex may try to maintain an inappropriate relationship, but you must accept it's over and move on. They might turn up uninvited at events where you are. Or they suddenly join the same gym where you exercise or run into them in a shop. They might even stalk you physically or online, so make sure you're no longer friends with them on any of your social media accounts.

You will have to set boundaries in communicating with your ex. This is especially important if you still need to continue sharing, e.g., if you have children. Don't feel pressured to respond to contact from the narcissist immediately; do this at a time that feels comfortable for you. If you must communicate with them about the shared custody of children, you must work with a lawyer to compile a parenting plan.

Keep all your responses and communication brief and to the point. Don't start unnecessary conversations or provide lengthy answers. Narcissists tend to remember everything you tell them and then use it against you. For example, don't tell them anything about what happens in the home while the children are with you. If you've forgotten to help the kids with their homework assignment and they know about it, they could try to use it against you in the ongoing custody battle.

Don't endure abusive behavior after a breakup. Make it clear to them that abusive and disrespectful communication won't be tolerated. If you need to communicate with an abusive ex-spouse, do so through your lawyers.

Use the absence of your ex-partner to regain your strength and focus on your well-being. Enjoy the peace and personal growth that can come from this newfound freedom. Discover new hobbies, make time to enjoy yourself, and find yourself again.

Finding healthy ways to deal with and recover from stress would be best.

If you must deal with them, offer constructive criticism sandwiched between compliments. This approach can lead to more effective and less aggressive conversations. We know narcissists appreciate validation and attention; many like to be the center of attention.

However, to avoid fueling their desire for attention, limit face-to-face engagement. Instead, opt for written or electronic communication when possible. You want to prevent the possibility of confrontation or inadvertently giving the narcissist information you don't want them to have.

Sometimes, narcissistic ex-partners may resort to making threats when they feel defeated. These are often empty threats, but you should not take them lightly. Narcissists have been known to resort to stalking behavior. Keep your information as private as possible, and keep your eyes open when you're out and about. Ask for help if you need it.

Despite the challenges, try to avoid publicly humiliating your ex-partner. Respect can help keep the peace and allow you to get on with your lives. This is especially important when you have children and must set an example for them.

ACTIVITY – SETTING DIGITAL BOUNDARIES

Dealing with a narcissistic ex-partner can be challenging, but setting clear digital boundaries can help protect your emotional well-being.

Do the following exercises in your journal or on one of your digital devices:

Manipulative text messages

Look at manipulative or abusive texts that you have received from your narcissistic ex-partner. See if it contains examples of guilt-tripping, gaslighting, blame-shifting, and attempts to provoke emotional reactions.

Consider what effective responses to these texts could be and write them down.

Emotional triggers

Think about which types of messages from your ex-partner trigger emotional responses in you. If you understand your triggers, you can respond more thoughtfully.

Your digital boundaries

Create a list of digital boundaries you want to set with your ex. This could include only responding to a certain number of messages in a day and only doing so at certain times.

Digital empowerment

Develop a digital empowerment plan that outlines how you will implement your boundaries in real-life text conversations with your narcissistic ex-partner.

How will you communicate these boundaries to them, if necessary?

KEY TAKEAWAYS

- You need to protect your well-being after breaking up with a narcissist.
- Acknowledge that the relationship has ended and set boundaries when communicating with your ex.
- Protect your personal information that you don't want your ex to have access to.
- Take time to rediscover yourself after breaking up with your ex.

GLOSSARY

This glossary guides understanding the terminology relevant to narcissistic/toxic relationships.

Abuse cycle: This is a repetitive pattern of abusive behavior characterized by phases of tension building, an abusive incident, and a period of reconciliation. This cycle can continue endlessly and can trap the victim in the relationship.

Boundaries: Consider boundaries as invisible lines you draw around yourself to protect your feelings and well-being in a relationship. This is one of the most important things you can have in a toxic relationship. It's the rules for how you expect to be treated, and if you're treated in a hurtful way, you can take action to make sure it doesn't happen again.

Codependency: A simple way to explain this is to refer to a relationship where one person depends too much on the other person to feel good about themselves. The codependent person usually does everything they can to make the other person in the relationship happy. They'll continue to try to please the other person, even when it's not good for their mental and physical health.

Complex post-traumatic stress disorder (CPTSD): Imagine going through a relationship where you are mistreated for many years. CPTSD happens when your mind and body become overwhelmed by stress, and you can feel sad, scared, or even sick. You may have difficulty trusting others, get night-mares, and feel irritable.

Flying monkeys: These are people who, intentionally or not, help the narcissist. This isn't easy because it will feel like more than one person is against you. They will also use these people to get you back into the relationship.

Gaslighting: This happens when someone tries to make you believe that what you see, remember, or feel isn't authentic or genuine. It's like they're playing tricks on your mind to confuse you. You might even end up wondering if you're crazy. Narcis-sists use this technique to manipulate you by making you ques-tion your thoughts and feelings. It can harm your confidence and general well-being.

Hoovering: The narcissist mistreated you in the past and will try to make you feel close to them again after a while. They try to trick you back into a relationship with them, even if it wasn't good before. They promise they'll change and the relationship will improve, but it's soon just as bad as before. Be cautious and remember how they treated you before.

Love bombing: Narcissists shower you with gifts, compli-ments, and attention at the beginning of a new relationship. They'll make you feel special and as if you're the most amazing person in the world. This is a form of manipulation, as they don't genuinely care, but they're trying to trick you into the relationship. Soon after this, they will start to devalue you and mistreat you.

Narcissistic personality disorder (NPD): Narcissists think they are special people and constantly want to hear it from others. They're self-focused and crave compliments and attention, making them feel even more special. Narcissists also don't care about how others feel.

No contact (NC): NC is about creating a protective barrier between you and the narcissist. It's almost like building a wall to keep them away. The aim is also to cut off all forms of digital communication with them. While you have contact with a narcissist, there is always the danger that they can pull you back into the relationship.

Trauma bonding: The narcissists treat you poorly and hurt you emotionally, but then they apologize, and things are good for a while. This cycle of good and bad times keeps repeating. You find it very hard to leave the relationship, as you still have feelings for the person and feel stuck.

Walking on eggshells: If you're in a relationship with a narcissist, you know they are highly unpredictable and get upset for no apparent reason. You must always be careful how you react around them, as you're scared of how they might respond. You're trying to avoid doing anything that might make them explode, even though it's not your fault.

END-BOOK REVIEW PAGE

Spread Hope!

There is hope ahead of you, and as you continue forward on your path, you're in a wonderful position to help someone else.

Simply by sharing your honest opinion of this book and (only if you're comfortable) a little about your own experience, you'll show new readers exactly where to go to start their healing journey.

IN UNDER 1 MINUTE
YOU CAN HELP OTHERS JUST LIKE YOU BY LEAVING A REVIEW!

Thank you so much for your support. Keep going: There's a bright future ahead of you.

CONCLUSION

As we end our journey together, you have gained the courage and resilience to get healthy and overcome narcissistic abuse. You've come a long way from confronting your narcissistic abuser to taking steps to safeguard your well-being. You've faced your fears and emerged stronger and ready to thrive. You'll take on life, focusing more on achieving your goals and shaping your life how you want it. This book has hopefully made you realize that you don't simply have to live to satisfy the needs of others. You are important, too, and you deserve to live your life how you want.

If you feel you're not quite there yet, or you've read the book, but you're not ready to put the steps into practice, don't worry. By reading this book, you've already taken the all-important first step toward leaving your toxic relationship: educating yourself and researching. Be patient and kind to yourself when making these big, life-changing decisions under difficult circumstances. Give yourself time to breathe. You don't have to change your life overnight, especially when you're already experiencing a lot of stress. When dealing with a narcissist, it's better to take your time, carefully consider your options, and plan extensively before you leave them. Make sure to have some cash that they don't know about. This will help you a great deal when it comes to kickstarting your new life. You must consider your mental and physical safety and what will be best for you in the long term.

Narcissists are devious; there is the danger that they will try to punish you for leaving them, and this can be catastrophic if you aren't adequately prepared. If you fall for their manipulation (guilt-tripping and hoovering), you may find yourself back in the relationship before realizing how that happened.

This book looks at the dark heart of narcissistic abusers and the manipulation and dependency that have trapped many people. The insidious tactics of narcissists have been uncovered, and we've harnessed the transformative power of setting boundaries for the sake of your self-preservation. Trauma bonding and the long-term scars of narcissistic abuse were also discussed.

As you've learned, the healing part of this journey is letting go of the toxic relationship. Before you can do anything else, you have to acknowledge how destructive your relationship is and that the best thing you can do for your long-term overall health is to let it go.

The book also encourages you to rediscover your unique strengths and talents. We've shown you how to reconstruct your self-esteem and confidence. This has helped you realize you're not defined by the wounds you've suffered in the past. Your resilience has kept you through the toxicity and will allow you to move on to the next part of your life, especially when forming healthy relationships.

The main message of this book is the following: While recovery from narcissistic abuse is a complex and emotionally draining process, it's entirely possible with the proper support. The key takeaway is that you can break free from narcissistic abuse to lead a meaningful life.

It's important to realize that you're not going through this process alone and are not the first or last person to experience this type of abuse. You're part of a large community of survivors, and you can share your success story and experiences to inspire and uplift others if you want to do so.

Let me share a success story with you. Lauren was trapped in a toxic relationship with a narcissistic man who wasn't only emotionally manipulative but also abused her physically. It left her full of self-doubt, but she was determined to escape her abuser. She decided she deserved better and that her happiness was worth fighting for.

However, she faced an uphill battle as she had little money since her abusive partner had squandered her inheritance. She managed to put a little of her salary aside into a secret account for a few months, and then, one day, she decided she had enough. She packed her clothes and left the apartment when he wasn't home.

After Lauren managed to escape her abuser, she sought support from therapists and support groups, and through the therapeutic process, she learned to confront and process the trauma, cope with her emotional and physical scars, and gradually regain her sense of self.

Lauren managed to start a new relationship successfully, and today, she's happily married with two children. She also studied psychology, and she provides counseling to others who are struggling in toxic relationships.

Like Lauren, you also deserve a meaningful and peaceful life. You can choose not to be defined by your past but rather by the outcome of your remarkable healing journey.

As you set out to reclaim your life and walk forward into a new beginning, I invite you to share your success story with others on the same path. You can provide hope and inspiration to those looking for healing. However, this is entirely your choice, and you don't have to talk to others about your experiences if you don't want to do so.

I wish you a future filled with love, strength, and joy. You deserve the opportunity to lead a meaningful life, and it's never too late.

I have one last request. If you found this book valuable, please consider leaving a review to help others discover the path to recovery from narcissistic abuse.

Stay strong, and I wish you all the best for your continued recovery journey. Maybe you still have a way to go, but you will soon reach a place where life is better than you can ever remember.

ABOUT THE AUTHOR

Ember Bennett has completed her healing journey. Her experiences have inspired her to help as many people as possible to avoid the struggles and trauma of being in and leaving a toxic relationship.

REFERENCES

Arabi, S. (2016, May 31). *10 life-changing truths abuse survivors should embrace.* HuffPost. https://www.huffpost.com/entry/what-abuse-survivors-dont-know-10-life-changing-truths_b_574e0a96e4b0068c40dfa484.

Baghadia, N. (2020, December 31). *Here's how to perform a burning ceremony in 4 simple steps.* YouAligned™. https://youaligned.com/lifestyle/how-to-burning-ceremony/#:~:text.

Basu, T. (2022, June 20). *How to stop being codependent in a relationship—expert explains.* Bonobology.com. https://www.bonobology.com/how-to-stop-being-codependent/.

Being, G. (2021, November 17). *Stop being codependent with a narcissist | 5 Step Guide.* Grace Being. https://grace-being.com/love-relationships/how-to-stop-being-codependent-with-a-narcissist/#:~:text.

Bonlor, A. (n.d.). *What does a healthy relationship look like?* Psychology Today. https://www.psychologytoday.com/za/blog/friendship-20/201812/what-does-healthy-relationship-look.

Boudin, M. (2021, September 21). *11 quotes about narcissism from actual therapists.* Choosing Therapy. https://www.choosingtherapy.com/narcissist-quotes/.

Carl, S. (2015, July 16). *10 ways to discover your unique gift.* Passion in Education. https://www.passionineducation.com/10-ways-to-discover-your-unique-gift/.

Davies, S. (2019, November 27). *Healing from the trauma of narcissistic abuse.* Tiny Buddha. https://tinybuddha.com/blog/healing-from-the-trauma-of-narcissistic-abuse/.

Dawson, C. (2021, February 21). *How setting intentions is powerful for personal growth.* Written by Charlotte. https://writtenbycharlotte.com/setting-intentions-personal-growth/.

Fraser, R. (2021, October 14). *Narcissistic abuse survivor shares her inspiring story.* Stylist. https://www.stylist.co.uk/relationships/narcissistic-abuse-toxic-relationship/547141.

Gonsalves, K. (2022, December 21) *Is your partner a narcissist? Take this 5-*

minute test to find out. Mindbodygreen. https://www.mindbodygreen.com/articles/narcissist-test.

Hammond, C. (2018, March 24). 10 Strategies for Dealing with Your Narcissistic Ex. Psych Central. https://psychcentral.com/pro/exhausted-woman/2018/03/10-strategies-for-dealing-with-your-narcissistic-ex#2.

Hedger, S. (2012, May 27). *Real people real stories: I lived with a narcissist for 14 years!* Stephen Hedger. https://www.stephenhedger.com/real-people-real-stories-i-lived-with-a-narcissist-for-14-years/.

Heyl, J. (2023, May 12) *What is C-PTSD from narcissistic abuse?* Verywell Mind. https://www.verywellmind.com/c-ptsd-narcissistic-abuse-5225119.

Jones, J. (2022, January 4). *Journaling for recovery.* Broxtowe Women's Project. https://broxtowewomensproject.org.uk/journaling-for-recovery/.

McDonald, Jorie N. "36 Healing Quotes For Inspiration And Encouragement." Southern Living. Last modified June 6, 2023. https://www.southernliving.com/culture/healing-quotes.

Nestler, J. (2023, July 26). *Boundaries: An important key in healing from narcissistic abuse.* Kingdom Winds. https://kingdomwinds.com/boundaries-an-important-key-in-healing-from-narcissistic-abuse/.

Nichols, L. (2019, July 25). *Confidence after narcissistic abuse—4 tips to boost and rebuild.* Moving Forward with Hope. https://www.movingforwardafterabuse.com/confidence/.

Pattemore, C. (2021, June 3). *10 ways to build and preserve better boundaries.* Psych Central. https://psychcentral.com/lib/10-way-to-build-and-preserve-better-boundaries#10-tips.

Pencak, S. (2013, November 30). *How to discover gifts | How to be yourself & reach your potential.* Silvia Pencak. https://silviapencak.com/how-to-discover-gifts/.

Saeed, K. (2023, July 27). *Give your new relationship a fighting chance after narcissistic abuse.* Kim Saeed. https://kimsaeed.com/2023/07/27/give-your-new-relationship-a-fighting-chance-after-narcissistic-abuse/#:~:text.

Shaw, E. (2019, November 21). *Overcoming guilt after narcissistic abuse. Overcoming narcissistic abuse.* Elizabeth Shaw. https://wasitme.blog/2019/11/21/overcoming-guilt-after-narcissistic-abuse/.

Thomas, V. (n.d.). *Council post: Five ways to set boundaries with toxic people.* Forbes. https://www.forbes.com/sites/forbescoachescouncil/2020/01/31/five-ways-to-set-boundaries-with-toxic-people/?sh=34623e21d02c.

Top 10 journal prompts for narcissistic abuse. (2023, June 25). Ineffable Living. https://ineffableliving.com/journal-prompts-for-narcissistic-abuse/.

Van Dyke, K. (2021, August 20). *How to emotionally detach from someone.* Psych Central. https://psychcentral.com/lib/the-what-why-when-and-how-of-detaching-from-loved-ones.

VanDerBill, Brittany. "Narcissistic Abuse in the United States." Psych Central. Last modified March 29, 2022. https://psychcentral.com/health/how-common-is-narcissistic-abuse-in-the-united-states.

White, M. A. (2022, October 5). *Narcissistic abuse: Definition, signs, and recovery.* Medical News Today. *https://ww*w.medicalnewstoday.com/articles/narcissistic-abuse.

Williams, H. (2023, February 19). *What does a healthy relationship look like after narcissistic abuse.* Relation Rise. https://relationrise.com/what-does-a-healthy-relationship-look-like-after-narcissistic-abuse/.

www.ingramcontent.com/pod-product-compliance
Lightning Source LLC
Chambersburg PA
CBHW022057020426
42335CB00012B/731